OCR Cambridge Nationals in ICT

Unit R003

Handling Data Using Spreadsheets

Microsoft® Excel 2010

Created and published by:

CiA Training Ltd
Business & Innovation Centre
Sunderland Enterprise Park
Sunderland
SR5 2TA
United Kingdom

Tel: +44 (0) 191 549 5002
Fax: +44 (0) 191 549 9005
E-mail: info@ciatraining.co.uk
Web: www.ciatraining.co.uk

ISBN: 978-1-86005-984-1
Release: OCN02v1

Acknowledgements

Microsoft® is a registered trademark and *Windows*® is a trademark of the Microsoft Corporation. Screen images reproduced with permission. Any other trademarks that appear in this guide are acknowledged as the property of their respective owners.

Introduction

> Hello and welcome to *Big Planet Theme Park* – the world's first ICT amusement park. From high-speed rollercoasters to haunted castle rides, there really is something for everyone!

OCR Cambridge Nationals in ICT: Unit R003

The aim of this guide is to provide the knowledge and skills needed to achieve the optional *Cambridge Nationals in ICT* unit *Handling Data Using Spreadsheets* (R003). Building upon units R001 and R002, it features a range of step-by-step exercises and problem solving activities based in and around the fictional business *Big Planet Theme Park*.

As you progress through this guide you will be introduced to many of the more powerful features of *Microsoft Excel* and see how to use the application to complete a number of simple, everyday tasks. This helps to build confidence in the application's use and your own ability to enter, develop and organise numerical information for a variety of purposes. The practical skills learned can then be used to solve ICT problems in your own life – at home, in education and at work.

Enjoy your visit to *Big Planet Theme Park* and have fun!

Learning objectives

To get the most out of your own education and employment opportunities, you need to be able to use ICT confidently, effectively and independently. The *Cambridge Nationals in ICT* qualification seeks to give you that ability, providing the knowledge and skills needed to successfully use computing technology in all aspects of your daily life.

Remember that achieving a *Cambridge Nationals in ICT* qualification is not just about knowing how to use computing technology, but realising how to apply that practical knowledge to solve unfamiliar problems in every aspect of your life. Each of the 10 sections in this book are therefore based on authentic work-related scenarios drawn from real-world experiences, and each teaches a relevant set of skills that are highly valued in both further education and employment.

After completing this book you will be able to:

*   Solve real-world problems using appropriate spreadsheet software (*Microsoft Excel*)

*   Interpret requirements and create suitable spreadsheet solutions

*   Apply knowledge and skills to process, manipulate and analyse unstructured data

*   Use functions and outputs to communicate information and engage with others

*   Present information graphically to help make decisions

Software and data files

This guide was designed to be used with *Microsoft Excel 2010* running on *Windows 7*. If you are using a different version of *Office* or *Windows*, some features may look or function slightly differently to that described.

 Data files accompanying this book enable you to practice new skills without the need for lots of data entry. These files must be downloaded from our website. To do this, go to **www.ciatraining.co.uk/data** and follow the simple on-screen instructions.

Your *FastCode* for this book's data is: **OCN02**

The data files will be installed in the following location on your computer:

Documents \ DATA FILES \ OCR Cambridge Nationals \ Unit R003

Notation used

Key presses are included within angled brackets. For example, <**Enter**> means press the **Enter** key on your computer's keyboard once. Also, unless otherwise specified, clicking the mouse means click the *left* mouse button once.

Recommendations

Each section in this guide is split up into lots of individual exercises. Most exercises consist of a written explanation of a specific software feature or technique followed by a practical, stepped activity. As each activity builds upon and extends the last, it is important that you work through all of the exercises in sequence (if you do not, you may encounter data file problems).

Also try to read the whole of each exercise before starting to work through it. This aids the learning process and helps to prevent unnecessary mistakes.

Qualification summary

The *OCR Cambridge Nationals in ICT* (Level 1/2) is a vocational (work-related) qualification with three levels of achievement: **Award**, **Certificate** and **Diploma**. To obtain an Award you must successfully complete the qualification's two mandatory units (R001 and R002). To obtain a Certificate you must complete the two mandatory units plus two additional optional units. To obtain a Diploma, you must complete the two mandatory units plus six additional optional units.

Extra learning resources for other units of the *Cambridge Nationals in ICT* qualification are available from *CiA Training*. To find out more please visit our website: **www.ciatraining.co.uk**.

Section Contents

Section 1

Excel Fundamentals

By the end of this section you should be able to:

Demonstrate a Basic Understanding of Excel

Recognise Workbooks and Worksheets

Select Cells and Ranges

Rename Worksheets

Copy and Move Worksheets

Insert and Delete Rows and Columns

Change Column Widths and Row Height

Hide and Display Rows and Columns

1.1 Microsoft Excel: The Basics

Microsoft Excel is most commonly used to work with figures and is a perfect choice of application for any task that involves numbers. Once a spreadsheet has been set up correctly it can be used to perform a number of complex calculations quickly and accurately (and any results will be automatically updated when the data is changed). Typically, spreadsheets can be used to help with the following tasks:

* Maths problems, budgets and accounting

* Cash flows and forecasts

* Data analyses

A spreadsheet stores information in a grid of **cells**. These generally contain text, numbers or the *results* of formulas and are arranged in numbered **rows** (going *down* the screen) and lettered **columns** (going *across* the screen), forming a **worksheet**. One or more worksheets together are known as a **workbook**, the name *Excel* gives to a saved file.

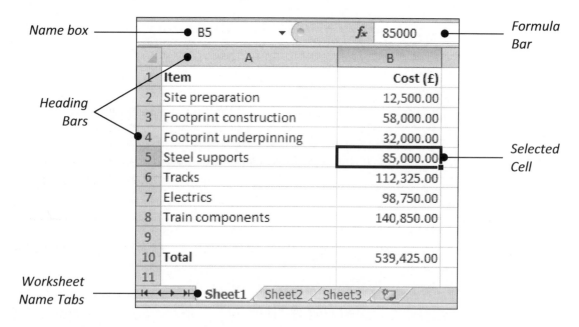

Notice the numbers running down the left side of the spreadsheet and the letters running across the top. These are called **Heading Bars** and are used to **reference** cells. In the picture above, the cell **B5** is currently selected (the location where **Column B** and **Row 5** intersect, as highlighted on the **Heading Bars**). This is known as the cell's **address** and is shown in the **Name** box.

> **Note:** When referring to a cell, the column letter <u>always</u> comes before the row number.

> **Note:** Although mainly used for working with numbers, people also use spreadsheets for creating and working with simple lists of data (e.g. product lists, stock lists, customer contact lists, etc).

Spreadsheets can also take basic data and present it in a variety of attractive graphs and charts. One important advantage of this is that the graphics created are much easier to understand at a glance. They can also be really useful for including in other documents or presentations.

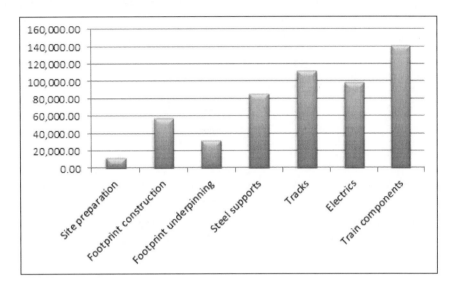

Activity:

1. Start *Microsoft Excel*. By default, a new blank workbook is created containing 3 empty worksheets: **Sheet1**, **Sheet2** and **Sheet3** (each with its own worksheet name tab).

Sheet Scroll Buttons
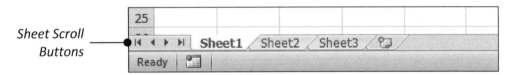

> **Note:**   If all the sheet name tabs cannot be displayed in the space available, then the sheet scroll buttons can be used to step horizontally through them.

2. Notice that cell **A1** is currently selected and appears with a dark border (it is the **active** cell). The **Heading Bars** for column **A** and row **1** are both highlighted.

> **Note:**   When creating a spreadsheet you should start on **Sheet1** and begin entering data in the top left corner. You should also add text **labels** to the top of columns or the start of rows to help describe their contents.

3. Type **First Quarter Finances** and press <**Enter**>. The active cell moves down to cell **A2**.

> **Note:**   The text in **A1** looks as though it also occupies cells **B1** and **C1**, but this is not the case. A label will expand and appear on top of other cells if – and only if – the other cells are empty. Cells containing numbers will not do this.

4. You can move to other cells by pointing and clicking or by using the arrow keys on your keyboard. Press the down arrow key <↓> to move to cell **A3**. Then, type **Property**.

> **Note:**   When entering a value into a cell notice that it also appears in the **Formula Bar**.

5.   Click once on cell **B3** to select it. Then type the number **25000** and press <**Enter**>.

	A	B	C
1	First Quarter Finances		
2			
3	Property	25000	
4			
5			

> **Note:**   In *Excel*, numbers (and the results of formulas) are also known as **values**.

> **Note:**   By default, labels appear left aligned and numbers appear right aligned. This helps you to tell at a glance which cells contain text and which contain values.

6.   Continue to enter data into the spreadsheet as shown below.

	A	B	C
1	First Quarter Finances		
2			
3	Property	25000	
4	Wages	200000	
5	Tax	20000	
6	Other	9250	
7			

7.   You have been informed that the contents of row **6** are not needed. Select cell **A6** by clicking it once using the mouse (or by moving to it using the arrow keys).

8.   Press the <**Delete**> key on your keyboard to remove the contents of the cell.

> **Note:**   The **Clear** button in the **Editing** group on the **Home** tab can be used to delete the contents of a cell and/or the text formatting applied to it.

9.   Select cell **B6**. This time, click the **Clear** button, in the **Editing** group. Then, select **Clear All** to remove the contents of the cell and any formatting.

> **Note:**   To save a workbook use the **Save** command on the **File** tab or the **Save** button on the **Quick Access Toolbar**.

10. Save the workbook as **finances** and leave it open for the next exercise.

1.2 Workbook Structure

A workbook can contain one or many worksheets (the name *Excel* gives to a spreadsheet), and each worksheet can be renamed, copied, moved or deleted.

Activity:

1. Default worksheet names are easy to change. Double-click the first worksheet name tab, **Sheet1**, to select the text. Then, type **First Quarter Finances** and press **<Enter>**. The worksheet has been renamed.

> **Note:** It is always good practice to give worksheets sensible and meaningful names which describe their contents. The sheet name tabs can contain up to 31 characters including spaces. Duplicate names, however, are not allowed.

2. Next, select **Sheet2** by clicking its worksheet name tab once. As no data has been entered here yet it is empty. Display **Sheet3** (which is also empty).

3. Click the **First Quarter Finances** tab again to return to the first sheet.

> **Note:** To remove an unwanted worksheet, right-click its name tab and select **Delete** or use the **Delete** button on the **Home** tab.

4. Right-click the **Sheet2** name tab to display a shortcut menu. Examine the options available and then select **Delete**. The sheet is permanently removed.

5. With **Sheet3** selected, click the drop-down arrow on the **Delete** button in the **Cells** group. Examine the options that appear and then select **Delete Sheet**.

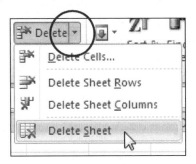

> **Note:** To add a worksheet to your workbook, click the **Insert Worksheet** button, .
> It is a good idea to keep all relevant worksheets in the same workbook.

6. Click the **Insert Worksheet** button found to the right of the **First Quarter Finances** tab.

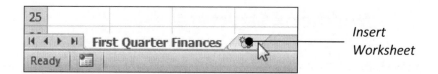

Insert
Worksheet

7. A new worksheet is created. Rename it as **Second Quarter Finances** and enter the values as shown below.

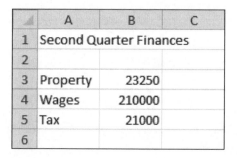

	A	B	C
1	Second Quarter Finances		
2			
3	Property	23250	
4	Wages	210000	
5	Tax	21000	
6			

> **Note:** To copy or move a worksheet, right-click its name tab and select **Move or Copy**.

8. Right-click the new **Second Quarter Finances** tab and select **Move or Copy**. The **Move or Copy** dialog box appears.

Create a Copy
Checkbox

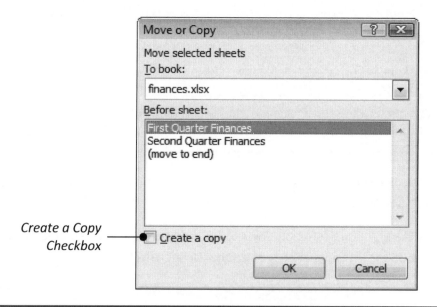

> **Note:** Notice that the current workbook file name is selected under **To book**. If necessary, you can also move or copy a worksheet to another *open* workbook.

9. To move the selected sheet *within the same workbook*, make sure **First Quarter Finances** is selected under **Before sheet**.

10. Click **OK**. The **Second Quarter Finances** tab now appears before the **First Quarter Finances** tab.

11. Right-click the **Second Quarter Finances** tab again and select **Move or Copy**. This time, place a check in the **Create a copy** box.

12. Next, select **(move to end)** under **Before sheet** to place a copy of the current worksheet at the end of the workbook.

13. Click **OK**. A new worksheet titled **Second Quarter Finances (2)** appears. Rename this to **Third Quarter Finances** and examine the sheet's copied contents.

> **Note:** You can change the contents of a cell by simply typing a new value when the cell is selected. However, when a cell entry is long or complicated, the changes are sometimes best made by editing the value in the **Formula Bar**.

14. Change the text in **A1** to **Third Quarter Finances**.

> **Note:** Worksheet name tabs can also be moved by dragging them.

15. Click and drag the worksheet title tab **First Quarter Finances** to the beginning of the worksheet list. Release the mouse button when the small downwards arrow, ▾, appears to the left of the **Second Quarter Finances** tab.

16. The worksheet is moved, as shown below.

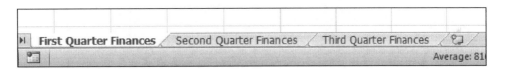

17. Finally, create a <u>copy</u> of the **Third Quarter Finances** worksheet and place it at the <u>end</u> of the workbook (i.e. after the first three worksheets).

18. Rename the new worksheet **Fourth Quarter Finances** and examine its copied contents. Change the value in **A1** to **Fourth Quarter Finances**.

> **Note:** Depending on your screen resolution, the worksheet title tabs may not all appear at the same time. If any are hidden, use the **Sheet Scroll Buttons**, ⏮ ◀ ▶ ⏭ , to view them.

19. Save the workbook using the same file name and close it.

1.3 Ranges

Ranges are rectangular collections of two or more *adjacent* cells (i.e. cells that are next to each other). They can be identified using *two* cell references separated by a colon (:) symbol: the *top left* cell in the range and *bottom right* cell. For example, the four cells **B2**, **B3**, **C2** and **C3** can be referenced by the range **B2:C3**.

Active Cell 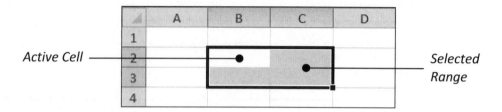 Selected Range

Activity:

1. Create a new, blank workbook.

> **Note:** To start a new workbook use the **New** command on the **File** tab.

2. Place the mouse pointer over cell **B2**. Then, click and drag down and to the right so that a range of six cells is highlighted, as shown below.

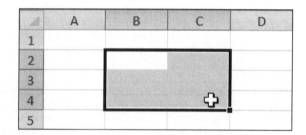

3. Release the mouse button. Notice that the first cell in the range remains white and the other cells are highlighted. The selected range can be referred to as **B2:C4**.

4. Selected ranges can be increased and decreased in size. Hold down the <**Shift**> key and select cell **E7**. The range is increased (and can now be referred to as **B2:E7**).

5. Hold down the <**Shift**> key again and select cell **C3**. The range is decreased (and can now be referred to as **B2:C3**).

6. Click anywhere on the worksheet to deselect the highlighted range.

> **Note:** More than one range can be selected at a time.

7. Select the range **B2:C4** again.

8. This time, press and hold down the <**Ctrl**> key and click and drag to select the range **D6:E8**. Release the <**Ctrl**> key. There should now be two separate ranges selected.

Select All ──
Button

9.   Click anywhere on the sheet to remove the selected ranges.

10. To select *all* the cells in a worksheet, click the **Select All** button, ☐, found to the left of the column **Heading Bar**.

> **Note:**   As you will find out in the next section, it is useful to be able to select ranges when formatting cell contents.

11. Click anywhere on the sheet to remove the selected range.

> **Note:**   As you will also later learn, ranges are used by most formulas and functions.

12. Close the workbook but leave *Excel* open for the next exercise.

1.4 Resizing Rows and Columns

You may sometimes need to change row heights and column widths to better display the contents of cells and to make your spreadsheets easier to read. This can be done by simply dragging the row or column **Heading Bar** borders.

Activity:

1.   Open the workbook **Attractions** which contains theme park ride statistics.

2.   Notice that the **Refurbished** title label in **D4** is slightly *truncated* (i.e. partly hidden by the contents of the next cell). Move the mouse pointer to the <u>border</u> between **D** and **E** on the column **Heading Bar**. The pointer should change shape to a double arrow, ✛.

> **Note:**   Width is measured in both number of characters (20.00 will show 20 standard characters) and pixels. These appear in a **ToolTip** when dragging.

3.   Click and drag the border to the right. When the column width is **13.00** (**96** pixels) release the mouse button.

> **Note:**   An alternative way to specify an exact row/column size is to use the **Row Height** and **Column Height** dialog boxes.

4.   On the column **Heading Bar**, click on **A** to select all of the cells in that column.

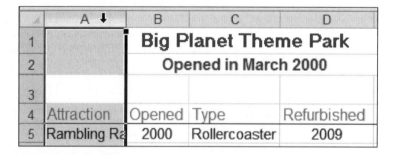

5.   Then, with the **Home** tab displayed, click the **Format** drop-down button in the **Cells** group and select **Column Width**. Enter a **Column width** of **22** and click **OK**. The column is changed to **22** units wide.

> **Note:**   A useful technique to automatically adjust the width of a column to accommodate all values contained within is to double-click its *right* border on the **Heading Bar**.

6.   Notice that the title label in **E4** is too large to fit within one cell. Move the mouse pointer to the border between **E** and **F** on the column **Heading Bar** and double-click. The width of column **E** is adjusted to the widest entry in that column (this is known as **AutoFit**).

> **Note:** You can change the height/width of many rows/columns at the same time.

7.   On the column **Heading Bar**, click and drag from **A** to **E** to select all 5 columns at once.

8.   With the columns **A** to **E** highlighted, drag any selected columns' *right* border to a width of **25** units. All the columns change to **25** units wide.

9.   Some of the columns are now too wide. With columns **A** to **E** still highlighted, double-click any selected columns' *right* border on the **Heading Bar**. All are "autofit" to the width of the widest entry in each column.

10. Row height is changed using similar techniques. Move the pointer to the border between **4** and **5** on the row **Heading Bar**. The pointer should change shape to a double arrow, ✛.

11. Drag the border down. When the row height is **18.00** (or **24** pixels) release the mouse button. The row is resized.

12. On the row **Heading Bar**, click and drag from **5** to **19** to select all 15 rows at once. Then, drag any of the selected rows' *bottom* borders to approximately **17** units.

13. Finally, using the row **Heading Bar**, click on **1** to select all of the cells in that row.

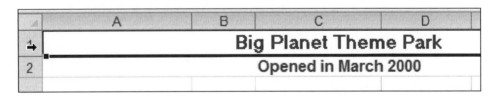

> **Note:** Non-adjacent rows and columns (i.e. rows and columns that are not next to each other) can also be selected by holding down **<Ctrl>** and clicking.

14. With the **Home** tab displayed, click the **Format** drop-down button in the **Cells** group and select **Row Height**. Enter a **Row height** of **24** and click **OK**.

> **Note:** Right-clicking **Heading Bars** displays a shortcut menu that also allows you to set row heights and column widths.

15. Well done. The spreadsheet is now neatly formatted and appears much more professional. Save it as **park attractions** and close it.

> **Note:** Use **Save As** on the **File** tab to save a workbook with a different file name.

1.5 Hiding Rows and Columns

Rows and columns can be temporarily hidden from view. This is useful if a spreadsheet contains sensitive information (e.g. salary details) that you might want to keep private, or simply if you want to "collapse" a lot of data into a smaller space.

Activity:

1. Open the workbook **Payroll** which shows salary payments for some of the park's workers.

2. Select all of column **G** (which refers to **Zahra**) using the column **Heading Bar**.

3. To hide this entire column, click the **Format** drop-down button in the **Cells** group. From the options that appear, select **Hide & Unhide | Hide Columns**. Column **G** is now hidden.

E	F	H	I
Yan	Julia	John	
£12.25	£20.50	£15.50	
37	35	35	

4. To redisplay column **G**, select **F** and **H** together using the column **Heading Bar**.

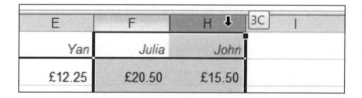

5. Then, click the **Format** drop-down button again. This time select **Hide & Unhide | Unhide Columns**. The hidden column reappears.

> **Note:** Right-clicking **Heading Bars** displays a shortcut menu that also allows you to hide and unhide rows and columns.

6. Using the row **Heading Bar**, right-click on **2** and select **Hide**. All of row **2** is now hidden.

7. To redisplay row **2**, select rows **1** to **3** on the row **Heading Bar**. Then, right-click the selection and click **Unhide**. The hidden row reappears.

> **Note:** Rows and columns may also be hidden by dragging their borders until the column width or the row height is zero. Dragging further hides multiple rows/columns.

> **Note:** You can also hide/unhide many selected rows/columns at the same time.

8. Leave the workbook open for the next exercise.

1.6 Editing Rows and Columns

When developing spreadsheets you will often need to create a new row or column within your data. Rows are inserted above the active cell and columns are inserted to the left. Similarly, rows and columns can also be deleted if they are no longer needed.

Activity:

1. The **Payroll** workbook should still open. Data for one of the park's employees, *Fiona*, needs to be added to the spreadsheet. Her payroll information should appear immediately <u>after</u> *Hassan's*.

2. Select all of column **C** using the **Heading Bar**. Then, click the **Insert** button, Insert (not the button's drop-down arrow) in the **Cells** group. The column containing *Priti's* payroll information is promoted to column **D** and a new column **C** is inserted.

3. Enter the label *Fiona* in cell **C1**. By default, an inserted cell copies the formatting of the cell immediately to the left.

4. Enter *Fiona's* payroll information as follows:

Fiona	
Hourly Rate	£12.00
Normal Hours	35
Hours Worked	37
Tax Code	800L

5. Data for employee overtime also needs to be added above **Tax Code**. Select all of row **5** using the **Heading Bar** and then click the **Insert** button in the **Cells** group. The row containing tax code information is promoted to row **6** and a new row **5** inserted.

6. Enter the row label **Overtime** in the empty cell **A5**. Then enter the following overtime information as follows:

Overtime	
Hassan	0
Fiona	2
Priti	3
Zak	5
Yan	3
Julia	0
Zahra	0
John	0

> **Note:**   When entering information into a spreadsheet, it is extremely important that you take care and avoid making mistakes. A spreadsheet that contains errors is of little use and the results generated will not be reliable or fit-for-purpose.

7. The **Normal Hours** row is no longer needed. Select all of row **3** using the **Heading Bar**.

8. Click the **Delete** button, ⊟ Delete , in the **Cells** group. The row is removed and all cells below moved up to occupy the space.

9. Removing columns uses the same technique. Select all of column **E** using the **Heading Bar** and then click the **Delete** button in the **Cells** group. The column is removed and all cells to the right moved left to occupy the space.

10. *Zak's* payroll information was deleted in error. Use the **Undo** button, ↺ , on the **Quick Access Toolbar** to reverse the deletion.

	A	B	C	D	E	F	G	H	I
1	*Payroll*	Hassan	Fiona	Priti	Zak	Yan	Julia	Zahra	John
2	Hourly Rate	£8.00	£12.00	£12.75	£10.75	£12.25	£20.50	£8.25	£15.50
3	Hours Worked	37	37	40	42	40	35	20	35
4	Overtime	0	2	3	5	3	0	0	0
5	Tax Code	300L	800L	367L	300L	300L	375H	300L	350L
6									
7	National Ins	10							
8	Income Tax	20							
9	Overtime Rate	1.25							
10									

> **Note:**   Right-clicking **Heading Bars** displays a shortcut menu that also allows you to add and delete selected rows and columns.

11. Using whichever technique you prefer, remove column **F** (*Yan*) and then delete row **7** (*National Ins*).

> **Note:**   The **Clear** button, ✐ , in the **Home** tab's **Editing** group, can be used to remove the contents of the selected row/column *without* deleting the cells.

> **Note:**   When selected, entire rows and columns can also be cut, copied and pasted using the familiar buttons in the **Clipboard** group on the **Home** tab.

12. Save the workbook as **payroll edited** and close it.

1.7 Develop Your Skills

At the end of every section you will find a *Develop Your Skills* activity. Work through it to ensure you have fully understood the previous exercises and can demonstrate the practical skills learned.

1. Open the workbook **Haunted**. *Zak* from the *Haunted Castle*, who is responsible for his engineering team's budget, has prepared this spreadsheet for last year's accounts.

2. *Zak* has forgotten to enter some of the figures in the **Other Income** row (row **9**). Enter the values as shown below:

Month	Amount
Feb	11
Apr	25
Aug	8
Oct	22
Nov	13

3. The **Demon of the Deep** was redesigned in May for the summer season. The total cost of the new equipment was £185,000, so change the value in **F12** to **185**.

4. Rename the <u>worksheet</u> (not the workbook) as **Haunted Castle Accounts**.

5. Increase all of the cells in column **A** to **15** units wide (**110** pixels).

6. Reduce columns **B** through to **M** to **7** units wide (**54** pixels).

7. Change the label in cell **A9** to **Additional**.

8. The wages information is very sensitive and should be *hidden* from view (<u>not deleted</u>). Hide all of row **11**.

9. Row **17** is not necessary and does not contain any useful information. Delete it.

10. Extra advertising money was spent in November in an attempt to boost visitor numbers during the winter months. Change the November (**Nov**) advertising cost to **12**.

11. You only want to see the final quarter of accounts. <u>Hide</u> columns **B** through **J**.

12. Save the workbook as **haunted third quarter** and close it.

> **Note:** A model solution for this activity is provided in the **Sample Solutions** data folder.

1.8 Section Summary

Well done! You have now completed all of the exercises in *Section 1: Excel Fundamentals*. Using the practical knowledge and skills learned you should now be able to:

- Demonstrate a basic understanding of *Microsoft Excel* and workbook structure

- Appreciate the importance of sheet names and row/column titles to describe a worksheet's contents

- Select individual cells and ranges

- Enter, edit and delete data in cells

- Rename worksheets

- Move and copy worksheets

- Insert and delete rows and columns

- Hide and unhide rows and columns

- Resize row height and column width

Note: If you feel you are unsure about any of the topics covered in this section, you should revisit the appropriate exercises and try them again before moving on.

Section 2

Formatting Cells

By the end of this section you should be able to:

Apply General Formatting

Format Numbers

Change Font, Font Size and Colour

Use Alignment

Use Text Wrap

Merge Cells

Add Borders and Shading

Use Conditional Formatting

2.1 Basic Formatting

Formatting cells can improve the appearance of worksheets and make it quicker and easier to understand the information they contain. To help emphasize important cells, standard text formatting techniques can be applied.

Activity:

1. Open the workbook **Sales**. This rather bland and uninteresting spreadsheet shows the total number of sales made by members of the theme park's *Gift Shop*.

2. Let's apply a little formatting to improve the look of the spreadsheet. First, select cell **A1**.

3. Then, click the **Bold** button, **B**, in the **Font** group on the **Home** tab. All of the text in the cell is made bold.

> **Note:** When formatting is applied to a cell, the button is toggled (i.e. switched on or off) in the **Font** group.

4. Next, click the **Underline** button, **U**, to underline the text. Click away from the cell to see the results more clearly.

> **Note:** A number of cells can be formatted at the same time by highlighting the required range first.

5. Select the range **B3:H3**. Then, click the **Italic** button, *I*, to italicise all of the selected cells.

6. Using the same technique, make the cells **A4:A8** italic also. Click away from the cells to see the results more clearly.

	A	B	C	D	E	F	G	H
1	**Gift Shop Sales**							
2								
3		*Mon*	*Tue*	*Wed*	*Thu*	*Fri*	*Sat*	*Sun*
4	*Hassan*	16	12	9	13	20	17	20
5	*Clare*	16	16	19	15	19	10	16
6	*John*	12	19	15	14	17	21	20
7	*Anton*	10	10	18	18	21	22	15
8	*Alya*	12	16	12	11	24	14	22

> **Note:** To only format parts of a cell's contents, select the appropriate text in the **Formula Bar** first or double-click the cell to perform **in-cell editing**.

7. Double-click cell **A11** to start in-cell editing. A cursor appears flashing within the cell.

8. Using the mouse, select the text **over 15** and click the **Bold** button. Then, select the text **10% bonus** and click the **Underline** button.

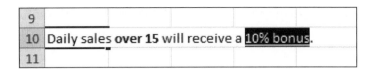

9. Click away from the active cell to see the results more clearly.

> **Note:** Standard **Font** type, size and colour settings can also be applied to cell contents.

10. Click the **Select All** button, [ ], found to the left of the column **Heading Bar**.

11. To change the font type, click the drop-down button on the **Font** box.

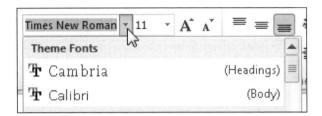

12. Locate and select **Calibri**. The font type for all selected cells is changed.

13. Next, click the drop-down button on the **Font Size** box (found to the right of **Font**) and select a size of **12**. The font size is changed.

14. Now, select cell **A1**. Then, click the **Font Color** drop-down arrow.

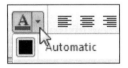

15. Move your mouse pointer over any colour in the palette to see the change automatically previewed on the spreadsheet. Finally click a dark blue colour to select it.

16. Using the **Font Size** drop-down, select a size of **16** (a good size for a worksheet's title).

> **Note:** Notice that the row's height is automatically increased to accommodate the text.

17. Finally, select the ranges **B3:H3** and **A4:A8** and choose a dark blue colour using the **Font Color** drop-down.

> **Note:** You can click the **Font Color** button to apply the most recently used colour again.

18. Click away from the select ranges to see the effect.

19. Save the workbook as **sales formatted** and leave it open for the next exercise.

2.2 Cell Alignment

Alignment refers to the positioning of text or numbers within a cell. Content can be aligned to any side of a cell and can even be rotated.

Activity:

1. Examine the buttons in the **Alignment** group on the **Home** tab. There are a number of options here to adjust the position of a selected cell's contents.

2. Using the **sales formatted** workbook saved in the previous exercise, select the range **B3:H3**. The selected cells' contents are currently left aligned (the default).

3. Click the **Center** button, to centre align the labels.

4. Next, select the range **A4:A8** and right align the cell contents using the **Align Text Right** button,

5. Now, select the range **B4:H8** and **Center** the values.

6. Using the row **Heading Bar**, select rows **3** to **8** together. Then, set the row height to **21.00** units (28 pixels) to make the information a little easier to read.

> **Note:**   You can also align a cell's contents *vertically* (up and down) as well as *horizontally*.

7. With rows **3** to **8** still selected, notice that **Bottom Align**, is toggled in the **Alignment** group. Similarly, the selected cell contents are aligned to the bottom of each cell.

8. Click the **Top Align** button, and observe the effect. Then, select **Middle Align**, to centre the cell contents vertically.

9. Click away from the selected range to see the effect.

	A	B	C	D	E	F	G	H
1	**Gift Shop Sales**							
2								
3		Mon	Tue	Wed	Thu	Fri	Sat	Sun
4	Hassan	16	12	9	13	20	17	20
5	Clare	16	16	19	15	19	10	16
6	John	12	19	15	14	17	21	20
7	Anton	10	10	18	18	21	22	15
8	Alya	12	16	12	11	24	14	22

> **Note:**   Cell contents can also be rotated to appear in the cell at different angles.

10. Increase the height of row **3** to **42** units (56 pixels) high. Then, select the range **B3:H3**.

11. Click the **Orientation** button, , and, from the drop-down list that appears, select **Vertical Text**.

12. Observe the effect. Then, click the **Orientation** button again. This time, select **Rotate Text Up**. Similarly, try **Rotate Text Down**.

13. Finally, select **Angle Counterclockwise**.

> **Note:** For more precise control over the alignment and rotation of cell contents, the **Format Cells** dialog box can be used.

14. With the range **B3:H3** still selected, click the **Format** button in the **Cells** group and select **Format Cells**. The **Format Cells** dialog box appears.

15. Select the **Alignment** tab and examine the options available. Expand the **Horizontal** and **Vertical** drop-down boxes to see additional alignment options.

16. Notice the **Orientation** settings. Using the up/down spinners (or by changing the value by overtyping), you can specify an exact rotation.

45	Degrees

17. The current rotation value of **45 Degrees** is fine. Click **OK** to close the dialog box.

18. Click away from the selected range to see the effect.

		Mon	Tue	Wed	Thu	Fri	Sat	Sun
2								
3								
4	*Hassan*	16	12	9	13	20	17	20

> **Note:** Rotating cell contents is often useful if you need to reduce the horizontal space occupied by column labels.

19. Save the workbook and leave it open for the next exercise.

> **Note:** Used properly, text formatting and alignment can highlight important information and give your spreadsheets a more professional appearance. However, too many different fonts, colours and styles can often have the reverse effect.

2.3 Borders and Fills

Borders are lines around the edges of individual cells or ranges. You can control the style and colours of the lines used and even apply **fills** to add a background shade or pattern.

Activity:

1. Using the **sales formatted** workbook, select the range **A4:A8**.

2. To apply a single black border around all cells in the selected range, click the drop-down arrow on the **Borders** button in the **Font** group.

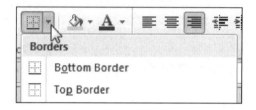

3. A large list of border settings appears. Choose the **All Borders** option, ⊞, to add a single black line to all edges. Click away from the selected range to see the effect.

4. Select the range **A4:A8** again. Then, drop down the **Borders** button and click **No Border**, ⊞, to remove all borders from the selected range.

> **Note:** The **Borders** button is useful for applying a quick border. However, for more control, the **Formal Cells** dialog box can again be used.

5. With the range **A4:A8** still selected, click the **Borders** button again. This time, select **More Borders**, ⊞, from the bottom of the drop-down. The **Format Cells** dialog box appears.

6. With the **Border** tab displayed, examine the options available.

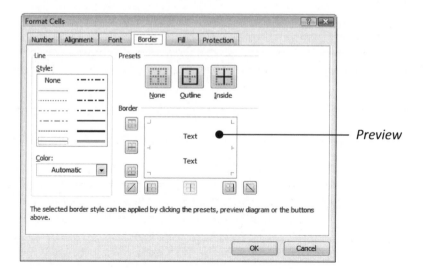

Preview

7. Notice the various border line styles available under **Style**. A single black line is selected by default and **Color** is set to **Automatic** (which, by default, is black).

> **Note:** Border **Line Style** and **Color** must be selected <u>first</u> before being applied.

8. Let's apply a thick, dark blue border to all cells. Select the double-thickness line within **Style**, then choose a **Dark Blue** colour from the **Color** drop-down (as shown below).

9. Next, click both the **Outline** and **Inside** buttons under **Presets** to apply a border *around* and *within* the selected range of cells. Notice the changes to the **Border** preview.

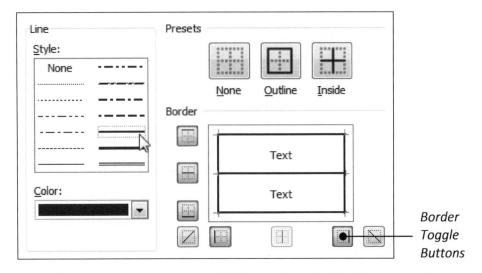

> **Note:** Notice that **Top**, **Middle**, **Bottom**, **Left** and **Right** border toggle buttons are active.

10. To apply the border click **OK**. Click away from the selected range to view the change.

11. Using the same technique, apply an identical border to the range **B3:H3**. Notice that the border appears at an angle matching the rotated contents of the selected cells.

12. Next, select the range **B4:H8** and display the **Format Cells** dialog box again. Notice that the **Border** preview already shows borders at the left and top of the selected range, as created earlier, and the preview's **Top** and **Left** border toggle buttons are active.

13. Select a single, thin solid line (————) under **Style** and **Green** from the **Color** drop-down. Then, click the **Bottom** and **Right** toggle buttons within the **Border** preview to apply the border style to those edges only.

14. Next, select a thin, dashed line (------------) under **Style**. Then, toggle both the horizontal and vertical **Middle** buttons within the **Border** preview to apply the border style.

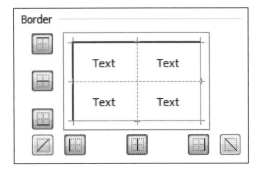

15. Click **OK** to apply the new border settings. A solid green line appears at the bottom and right of the selected range, with a dashed green line between cells. You can click away from the selected range to see the effect.

> **Note:** Borders can often be seen better if the worksheet's gridlines are hidden. To do this, select the **View** tab and uncheck **Gridlines** in the **Show** group. Be sure to check **Gridlines** again before continuing.

16. Shading is added to cells using either the **Fill Color** button, 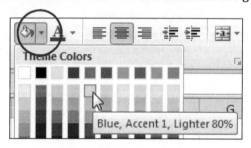, or the **Format Cells** dialog box. Select the range **B3:H3** again and make sure the **Home** tab is displayed.

17. Click the drop-down arrow on the **Fill Color** button and select a light blue colour.

> **Note:** It is often best to fill cell backgrounds using light colours; darker colours can obscure the text and make it difficult to read.

18. Apply the same light blue colour to the range **A4:A8**.

19. You can also fill cells with impressive gradient effects. Select the range **B3:H3** and display the **Format Cells** dialog box again. On the **Fill** tab, click **Fill Effects**.

20. In the **Color 1** drop-down box, select **White**. In the **Color 2** drop-down box, select the same light blue colour used earlier. Examine the **Shading styles** options and then click **OK**.

21. Click **OK** again to apply the fill. The spreadsheet should now look like that shown below.

	A	B	C	D	E	F	G	H	I
1	**Gift Shop Sales**								
2									
3		Mon	Tue	Wed	Thu	Fri	Sat	Sun	
4	Hassan	16	12	9	13	20	17	20	
5	Clare	16	16	19	15	19	10	16	
6	John	12	19	15	14	17	21	20	
7	Anton	10	10	18	18	21	22	15	
8	Alya	12	16	12	11	24	14	22	
9									

22. Save the workbook using the same file name and close it.

2.4 Text Wrap

Text Wrapping is used to fit data into cells without the need to change column widths or cell orientation. When applied, text that may normally appear truncated (i.e. partly hidden by the contents of adjacent cells) will be shown on more than one line instead.

Activity:

1.   Open the workbook **Breakdowns**. This spreadsheet contains an account of all ride failures that occurred last year at the *Haunted Castle*.

2.   Notice that some of the text in cell **A12** has been hidden by the contents of cell **B12**. To correct this, first select cell **A12**.

3.   To apply text wrapping, click the **Wrap Text** button, 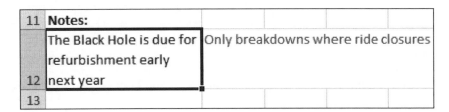, in the **Alignment** group. The text now appears on multiple lines and the row's height is automatically increased.

11	**Notes:**	
12	The Black Hole is due for refurbishment early next year	Only breakdowns where ride closures
13		

> **Note:**   Text wrapping can also be controlled using the **Format Cells** dialog box.

4.   With cell **A12** still selected, use the **Format** button in the **Cells** group to display the **Format Cells** dialog box. Select the **Alignment** tab and notice that **Wrap text** is now selected under **Text control**.

5.   Remove the check from the **Wrap text** box and click **OK**. Text wrapping is removed and the row's height automatically decreased.

6.   Using either the **Wrap Text** button or the **Format Cells** dialog box, apply text wrapping to cell **A12** again.

7.   Finally, apply text wrapping to cell **A14**.

8.   Save the workbook as **breakdowns edited** and leave it open for the next exercise.

2.5 Merge Cells

A range of cells can be **merged** into one, larger, single cell. This is particularly useful for creating spreadsheets where labels span across multiple columns or rows.

Activity:

1. Using the **breakdowns edited** workbook saved in the previous exercise, select the range **B1:M1**. You will now merge these cells and centre-align their contents.

2. Click the **Merge & Center** button, 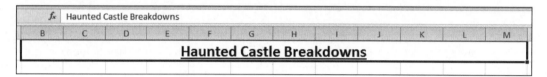, in the **Alignment** group (<u>not</u> the button's drop-down arrow). All 12 cells are merged into one and the text label centred.

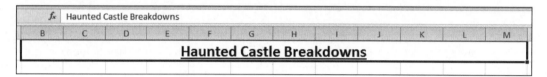

> **Note:** Notice that the **Merge & Center** button is now toggled.

3. To unmerge the selected cells, click the **Merge and Center** toggle button again.

4. With the range **B1:M1** still selected, display the **Format Cells** dialog box. On the **Alignment** tab, notice the **Merge cells** checkbox under **Text control**.

5. Place a check in the **Merge cells** checkbox and click **OK**. The cells are again merged but the label is not automatically centered.

6. Use the **Center** button in the **Alignment** group to manually centre the cell's contents.

7. Next, select the range **B12:M12**. Then, click the small drop-down arrow on the **Merge** button.

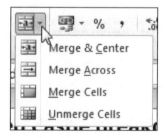

8. From the options that appear, select **Merge Cells**. Use the **Alignment** buttons again to horizontally and vertically align the text in the centre of the merged cells.

9. Save the workbook with the same file name and close it.

2.6 Number Formats

Cells can be formatted so that their contents are displayed in different ways, such as currency, percentages, dates, times, etc. The most useful number formats available include:

General	No specific number format (best for most uses)
Number	Plain number formats
Currency	Currency symbols and decimal places
Date	Various date formats
Time	Various time formats
Percentage	A value as a fraction of 100 (followed by %)
Fraction	Decimals expressed as fractions
Text	Plain text with no number formatting

> **Note:** When choosing a number format it is important to realise that the value in each cell is not changed. It is simply displayed in a different way.

Activity:

1. Open the workbook **Statistics**. This worksheet contains a number of interesting statistics for *Big Planet Theme Park*.

> **Note:** All cells in this spreadsheet currently use the **General** number format (the default). This means that text and numbers appear without any special formatting.

2. Although **General** is usually fine for text labels, cells that contain numbers will often benefit from having an appropriate format selected. Let's try this now.

3. Select the range **B4:B15**. These cells contain integers (whole numbers) and should be formatted as such. Click the **Format** button in the **Cells** group and select **Format Cells**.

4. Display the **Number** tab. Click on each of the different types of cell formatting shown in the **Category** list to see the various types and options available. Finally, select **Number**.

5. Change the number of **Decimal places** to **0** and place a check in the **Use 1000 Separator** box.

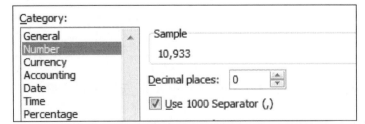

> **Note:** Notice the **Sample** preview. This shows the results of the chosen format as applied to the *first* number in the selected range.

6. Click **OK** and observe the effect.

> **Note:**   The **Number Format** button in the **Number** group, [Number ▾], can be used to select new formats quickly and easily.

7. With **B4:B15** still selected, notice that the **Number Format** button shows that the cells have a format of **Number**. Select the range **C4:C15** and this changes to **General**.

8. Click the drop-down arrow on the **Number Format** button. Examine the various options available and then select **Currency**. Observe the effect.

> **Note:**   You can fine tune how cells display their contents using the **Format Cells** dialog box.

9. With **C4:C15** still selected, display the **Format Cells** dialog box again. Reduce the number of **Decimal places** to **0** and click **OK**. Values are now shown rounded up to the nearest whole number.

> **Note:**   In *Excel*, the date is stored as a large number that represents the number of days that have passed since January 1, 1900. This must be formatted to appear in a more recognisable form (e.g. 21 April 2012).

10. Select the range **D4:D15** and apply a **Number Format** of **Short Date**. Observe the effect, and then select a **Number Format** of **Long Date** to see the difference.

> **Note:**   Times are stored in *Excel* as decimal numbers between 0 and 1. The decimal .0 represents 00:00:00 and .99999 represents 23:59:59.

11. Apply a **Number Format** of **Time** to the range **E4:E15**.

12. Cells **F4:F15** currently contain decimals. To show these as fractions instead, select the range and apply a **Number Format** of **Fraction**.

13. Similarly, apply a **Number Format** of **Percentage** to the range **G4:G15**.

> **Note:**   There are buttons in the **Number** group on the **Ribbon** to **Increase Decimal** places and **Decrease Decimal** places. This is done one decimal place at a time.

14. Select the range **H4:H15** and apply a **Number Format** of **Number**.

15. Click the **Decrease Decimal** button, [.00 →.0], to reduce the number of decimal places shown to 1. Then click it again to show only whole, rounded numbers.

16. Save the workbook as **statistics formatted** and close it.

2.7 Conditional Formatting

It is possible to apply different formatting to cells depending on the values they contain. For example, a cell could be coloured red if it is below, above or equal to a certain value. This is called **conditional formatting**.

Activity:

1. Open the workbook **Stocks**. This spreadsheet contains a short list of items that are available to buy from *Pirate's Cove*.

2. It would be useful to know when stocks of items are either too high (>30) or too low (<5). To do this, conditional formatting can be used. Select the range **C4:C12**.

3. Notice the colours used in the **Warnings** column **E**. Then, with the **Home** tab displayed, click the **Conditional Formatting** button in the **Styles** group.

4. There are several types of preset formatting available from the list, but to see all possible formatting options select **New Rule**. The **New Formatting Rule** dialog box is displayed.

5. Select each rule type shown and examine the description, settings and styles of formatting that apply to each. When you are finished, select **Format only cells that contain**.

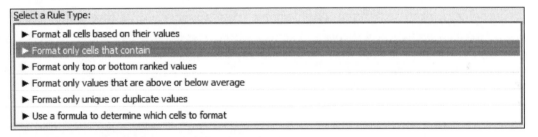

6. Examine the rule description. Then, click the drop-down arrow for the first box (currently containing **Cell Value**). Notice the various types of *criteria* that you can base your rule on.

7. Similarly, drop-down the second box and examine the various logical operators that you can apply. When you are finished, complete the new rule as shown below.

Note: This **Conditional Formatting** rule will be used to create an alert when stock is low.

---

8. Click the **Format** button. Notice that you can adjust the cell's font, border and fill. Select **Bold** from **Font style** and **White** from **Color**.

9. Next, display the **Fill** tab. Then, select **Red** for **Background Colour** and click **OK**. Notice the **Preview** that appears.

10. The rule is now complete. Click **OK** and observe the effect.

> **Note:** More than one rule can be applied at a time.

11. We're not finished yet! Recall that we also want to be notified when stocks get too high. Use the **Conditional Formatting** button to create a similar rule to the first with the following criteria:

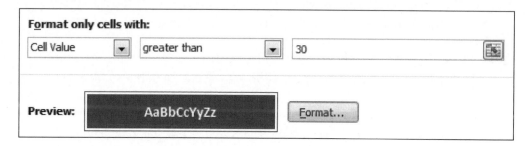

> **Note:** The colour **Purple** is used to highlight cells that are overstocked.

12. When you have created the new rule, click away from the selected range to see the effect. Stock quantities *lower than 5* now appear with white, bold text and a red background. Quantities *over 30* appear with white, bold text and a purple background.

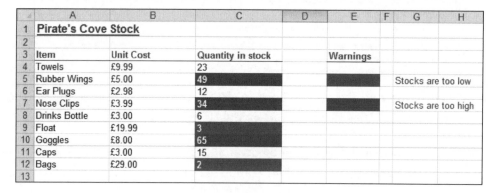

	A	B	C	D	E	F	G	H
1	**Pirate's Cove Stock**							
2								
3	Item	Unit Cost	Quantity in stock		Warnings			
4	Towels	£9.99	23					
5	Rubber Wings	£5.00	49					Stocks are too low
6	Ear Plugs	£2.98	12					
7	Nose Clips	£3.99	34					Stocks are too high
8	Drinks Bottle	£3.00	6					
9	Float	£19.99	3					
10	Goggles	£8.00	65					
11	Caps	£3.00	15					
12	Bags	£29.00	2					
13								

13. There has been a rush on **Rubber Wings**, with **22** selling in the last few minutes. Reduce the stock quantity for that item by changing the value in cell **C5** to **27**. The conditional rule is no longer true and so the formatting is not applied.

14. A stock check shows that there are fewer **Towels** available. Change the value in cell **C4** to **2**. The conditional rule now evaluates as true and so the formatting is applied.

> **Note:** Rules can be edited and removed using the **Conditional Formatting** button.

15. Experiment with changing values in column **C** and note how the condition formatting is applied. When you are finished, save the workbook as **stocks formatted** and close it.

2.8 Develop Your Skills

At the end of every section you will find a *Develop Your Skills* activity. Work through it to ensure you have fully understood the previous exercises and can demonstrate the practical skills learned.

1. Start a new, blank workbook.

2. Using the cell formatting techniques learned in this section, create the following timesheet for employees of the park to use.

> **Note:** Gridlines have been hidden by removing the check in the **Gridlines** box in the **Show** group on the **View** tab.

3. Format the range **C10:C16** using a **Number Format** of **Short Date**.

4. Similarly, format the ranges **D18:G18** and **D19:H19** using a **Number Format** of **Currency**. Make sure any future values entered will be shown to **2** decimal places.

5. Using **Conditional Formatting**, create a new rule which applies to the range **E10:E16**. If the value entered in any cells is *greater than 5*, fill the background with a light red colour.

> **Note:** It is always good practice to test that **Conditional Formatting** rules work as intended. Temporarily enter dummy data into cells to do this.

6. Save the workbook as **timesheet** and then close it.

> **Note:** A model solution for this activity is provided in the **Sample Solutions** data folder.

2.9 Section Summary

Well done! You have now completed all of the exercises in *Section 2: Formatting Cells*. Using the practical knowledge and skills learned you should now be able to:

- Format cells using basic text formatting techniques

- Apply appropriate number formats

- Change cell alignment

- Wrap text in cells

- Merge and unmerge cells

- Apply borders and shading

- Use conditional formatting

> **Note:** If you feel you are unsure about any of the topics covered in this section, you should revisit the appropriate exercises and try them again before moving on.

Section 3

Formulas

By the end of this section you should be able to:

Create Simple Formulas

Use Arithmetic Operators

Use Brackets to Force Order of Operation

Copy Formulas

Understand Relative and Absolute Addressing

Link Cells across Worksheets

Link Cells across Workbooks

3.1 Simple Formulas

Formulas can be used to perform simple calculations on the numbers in a spreadsheet. For example, they can be used to add a column or row of numbers together to obtain a total. If the numbers used in the calculation are changed, the formula will automatically recalculate the result.

> **Note:** All formulas begin with an equals sign (=), followed by a calculation.

Activity:

1. Open the workbook **Operations**. This spreadsheet has been created to demonstrate simple formulas for *adding*, *subtracting*, *multiplying* and *dividing* numbers.

> **Note:** Notice that each column uses a different **Number Format**: **General**, **Percentage**, **Currency** and **Number**. All number formats can be used in calculations.

2. First, to add the contents of **B4** and **B5** together, make **B6** the active cell by clicking on it. Then, type the following formula: **=B4+B5**.

	A	B	C	D	E
1	Mathematical Operations				
2					
3	Number	Add	Subtract	Multiply	Divide
4	First	21	64%	£33.20	168.32
5	Second	68	32%	£5.00	12.50
6	Result	=B4+B5			
7					

> **Note:** Notice that, as you type the formula, the referenced cells are highlighted in matching colours on the worksheet.

3. Press <**Enter**>. Cell **B6** now displays the <u>result</u> of the formula (**89**).

> **Note:** *Excel* will only do what you tell it to do. To produce valid results that are fit for purpose, always check that you use the correct operators in your formulas.

4. Select cell **B6** and notice that the **Formula Bar** displays **=B4+B5**, the formula for this cell.

5. Click in cell **B4** and enter **56** to overwrite the original contents. Press <**Enter**> and the formula automatically updates the result in **B6** to **124**.

6. Next, to subtract the contents of **C5** from **C4**, first make **C6** the active cell by clicking on it.

> **Note:** Clicking on cells to enter them in formulas is easier than typing and often reduces the chances of making a mistake.

7. Enter = to start a new formula. However, instead of typing the first cell reference, use your mouse to click once on cell **C4** to select it. It appears in your formula.

8. Next, enter the subtraction symbol, -, and then click on cell **C5**.

	A	B	C	D	E
1	**Mathematical Operations**				
2					
3	Number	Add	Subtract	Multiply	Divide
4	First	56	64%	£33.20	168.32
5	Second	68	32%	£5.00	12.50
6	Result	124	=C4-C5		

9. Press <**Enter**>. Cell **C6** now displays the <u>result</u> of the formula (**32%**).

> **Note:** Using the mouse to "build" a formula in this way is useful if you want to select and use a range of cells instead, as you will learn more about later.

10. In cell **D6**, enter the formula to multiply the two numbers in the cells above, **=D4*D5**. The result is **£166.00**.

> **Note:** It is usually quicker to use the numeric keypad on the right of a standard keyboard to enter large amounts of numbers. However, you may need to activate the **Number Lock** feature on your keyboard first by pressing <**Num Lock**> (a light on your keyboard will appear when it is activated).

11. In cell **E6**, enter a formula to divide the two numbers in the cells above, **=E4/E5**. The result is **13.47**.

	A	B	C	D	E
1	**Mathematical Operations**				
2					
3	Number	Add	Subtract	Multiply	Divide
4	First	56	64%	£33.20	168.32
5	Second	68	32%	£5.00	12.50
6	Result	124	32%	£166.00	13.47

> **Note:** Any calculations contained on a worksheet are unaffected by hiding rows/columns.

12. Save the workbook as **operations complete** and close it.

> **Note:** You will learn a lot more about formulas as you progress through this book.

3.2 Brackets

If more than one mathematical operation appears in a single formula, their order can be very important. For the four operations that you have seen so far, *Excel* performs calculations in this order: **Brackets**, **Division**, **Multiplication**, **Addition** and finally **Subtraction** (the **BODMAS** or **BIDMAS** rules in maths). As brackets come first, they can be used to force *Excel* to perform calculations in a specific order.

For example, in the formula **A1+A2/A3**, BODMAS states that the value in cell **A2** should be divided by **A3** first and then added to **A1**. However, brackets can be used to make sure **A1** is added to **A2** *first* before being divided by **A3**, as the following formula shows: **(A1+A2)/A3**.

Activity:

1.   Open the workbook **Pirates**. This spreadsheet has been created to demonstrate the effect of using brackets in your formulas.

> **Note:**   Although it is common practice to start creating spreadsheets from the upper left corner, you can in fact start in any cell you like.

2.   Examine the contents of the worksheet. Simple formulas are required to work out the profit from the sale of *Pirate's Cove* merchandise.

Gift Shop Sales: Pirate's Cove Merchandise			
T-shirts		*Baseball caps*	
Buy-in Price	£6.00	Buy-in Price	£7.50
No. Bought	10	No. Bought	10
Sale Price	£10.00	Sale Price	£12.99
No. Sold	3	No. Sold	7
Profit		Profit	

3.   To calculate the profit from the sale of *t-shirts*, the **Buy-in Price** must be subtracted from the **Sale Price** and then multiplied by the **No. Sold** (number sold). Click on cell **D12** and enter the formula **=d10-d8*d11**.

> **Note:**   *Excel* will automatically capitalise lower case (small) letters used in formulas.

4.   Press <**Enter**> to complete the formula. The answer given is **-£8.00**, which is not correct as each gift was sold for more than it was bought. Can you tell what has gone wrong?

5.   Due to the rules of *BODMAS*, the multiplication was carried out *before* the addition. Click on cell **D12** and press the <**Delete**> key to remove the formula.

6.   This time you will use brackets to make sure that the addition occurs first. Type in the formula **=(D10-D8)*D11** and press <**Enter**>.

7. Check that the result displayed is **£12.00** (the correct answer).

8. Next, use the same technique to calculate the total profit from all sales of *baseball caps*. The result obtained should be **£38.43**.

Profit	£12.00	Profit	£38.43

9. Select cell **G16**. To calculate the total value of all <u>remaining</u> stock, the **No. Sold** of *each item* must be subtracted from the **No. Bought** and then multiplied by the **Sale Price**.

10. Enter the following formula: **=D9-D11*D10+G9-G11*G10**.

=D9-D11*D10+G9-G11*G10

11. Press <**Enter**> and the result obtained is **-£100.93**. This does not look correct...

> **Note:** You should always check that formulas produce the expected results – it is very easy to make mistakes when building a spreadsheet and input errors are common.

12. The result is wrong as brackets were not used to force the correct order of operation. Select cell **G16** again – where should the brackets go?

13. To make sure *Excel* performs the calculations in the right order (i.e. the subtractions *before* the multiplication), edit the formula as follows: **=(D9-D11)*D10+(G9-G11)*G10**.

=(D9-D11)*D10+(G9-G11)*G10

14. The formula now subtracts **D11** from **D9** first, then **G11** from **G9**. Following the rules of BODMAS, the result of the first bracket is multiplied by **D10** and the result of the second bracket multiplied by **G10**. Finally, the two separate results are added together to produce **£108.97** (which is now correct).

> **Note:** When brackets appear inside of other brackets, the inside brackets are <u>always</u> calculated <u>first</u>.

> **Note:** Even when not required, it is often a good idea to use brackets to group operations and make their order absolutely clear.

15. Select cell **G16** again and edit the formula as follows: **=((D9-D11)*D10)+((G9-G11)*G10)**.

16. The result is the same as the order of operations has not changed. However, the formula is now a little clearer and easier to read and understand.

17. Save the workbook as **pirates complete** and close it.

3.3 Copying Formulas

A very useful feature of *Excel* is the ability to quickly and easily copy formulas to other cells. Importantly, any formulas that are copied and pasted will have all cell references <u>automatically changed</u> to suit their new locations, as you will see in this exercise.

> **Note:** Cell references are <u>not</u> adjusted when a formula is <u>cut</u> and pasted.

Formulas can also be copied to a range of <u>adjacent</u> cells (i.e. cells that are next to each other) by dragging the **Fill Handle**.

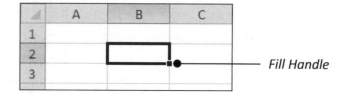

Fill Handle

Activity:

1. Open the workbook **Weekly Hours**. The worksheet titled **Week 1** contains a list of the hours worked by three employees of *Big Planet Theme Park*.

2. In cells **A8** and **H3**, enter the text label **Total**.

3. Click on cell **B8**. The cells containing numbers above need to be added together. Enter the formula **=B4+B5+B6** and press **<Enter>**. The answer should be **16**.

4. Click on cell **H4**. The cells containing numbers to the left also need to be added together to find the total. Enter the formula **=B4+C4+D4+E4+F4** and press **<Enter>**. The answer should be **28**.

> **Note:** You will learn how to create formulas much quicker in later exercises.

5. Select cell **B8** again and notice the contents of the **Formula Bar**.

6. To copy this formula to another cell, click the **Copy** button, , in the **Clipboard** group on the **Home** tab (or press **<Ctrl+C>**).

> **Note:** The copied cell appears with an animated border. The message **Select destination and press ENTER or choose Paste** is also displayed on the **Status Bar**.

7. Select cell **C8** and click the **Paste** button in the **Clipboard** group (or press **<Ctrl+V>** or **<Enter>**). The formula is copied from cell **B8** and pasted in **C8**.

8. Observe the contents of the **Formula Bar**. The copied formula has been automatically changed and now references cells in column **C** rather than **B**.

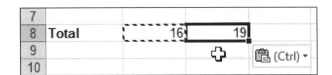

7			
8	Total	16	19
9			
10			

> **Note:** Notice that cell **B8** still has an animated border. This indicates that its contents can be pasted again if required.

9. Select the range **D8:F8** and click **Paste**. The copied formula is pasted into *all* cells in the range, with each instance updated to reference the cells above.

10. Select each cell in the range **D8:F8** in turn to observe the changes made to the formula in the **Formula Bar**.

> **Note:** You can double-click a cell containing a formula to begin in-cell editing and highlight the cells referenced by it.

11. Copy the formula in cell **H4** to the range **H5:H6**.

	A	B	C	D	E	F	G	H
1	Hours Worked (Week 1)							
2								
3	Employee	Mon	Tue	Wed	Thu	Fri		Total
4	Hassan	2	5	7	7	7		28
5	Fiona	8	8	2	5	2		25
6	John	6	6	6	8	5		31
7								
8	Total	16	19	15	20	14		

12. Select each cell again to observe the changes made to their formulas.

> **Note:** Formulas can also be easily copied to adjacent cells using the **Fill Handle**.

13. Display the worksheet **Week 2** by clicking its name tab once.

14. With cell **B8** selected, move your mouse pointer over the **Fill Handle**. The mouse pointer changes to a crosshair, **+**.

15. Click and drag the **Fill Handle** across to cell **F8**.

	A	B	C	D	E	F	G	H
1	Hours Worked (Week 2)							
2								
3	Employee	Mon	Tue	Wed	Thu	Fri		Total
4	Hassan	3	6	3	4	7		23
5	Fiona	4	5	2		2		
6	John	6	6	6	8			
7								
8	Total	13						
9								

16. Release the mouse and the formula in **B8** is copied to the range **C8:F8**.

Note: The fill handle can only be dragged horizontally (left/right) or vertically (up/down) in one direction at a time.

---

17. Use the **Fill Handle** to copy the formula in cell **H4** to the range **H5:H6**.

	A	B	C	D	E	F	G	H
1	Hours Worked (Week 2)							
2								
3	Employee	Mon	Tue	Wed	Thu	Fri		Total
4	Hassan	3	6	3	4	7		23
5	Fiona	4	5	2		2		13
6	John	6	6	6	8			26
7								
8	Total	13	17	11	12	9		
9								

Note: *Why add cells that contain nothing?* Well, if numbers were placed in these cells at a later stage then the formula would still work, but a formula with cells missing from the range would not.

---

18. Save the workbook as **weekly hours final** and close it.

3.4 Absolute Addressing

Normally the cell references that you use in your formulas are known as **relative** cell references; they are automatically updated by *Excel* when copied to another cell. For example, if you copy the formula **B2+B3** in column **B** to column **C** it automatically becomes **C2+C3**.

However, if you want to stop *Excel* automatically updating references you can use **absolute** cell referencing instead. To make a cell reference **absolute** you simply add a **$** symbol before the row and/or column identifier. For example, **$A$1** will *always* refer to cell **A1** wherever it is copied to.

Activity:

1. Open the workbook **Parts** which contains the start of a tax calculation. However, the VAT (Value Added Tax) calculations have not been completed yet.

> **Note:**   VAT is a government tax charged on most goods and services purchased in the UK.

2. Select cell **C6** and enter the formula for **VAT** (**Price** multiplied by the **VAT Rate**): =C5*B15.

3. Check that the result shown in cell **C6** is **£799.58**.

4. Next, select **B15** and change the **VAT Rate** to **20%** (you can enter this as **0.2** or **20%**). Notice that the result in **C6** is updated.

5. Use the **Fill Handle** to copy the formula in **C6** to both **D6** and **E6**. The resulting **VAT** for both cells is **£0.00**, which is clearly not correct. Check the formulas in **D6** and **E6**. Can you find the problem?

6. The error is a result of *relative* cell addressing. The **VAT Rate** value is only in cell **B15**, but the formulas have been automatically updated to reference cells that are empty (e.g. the cells **C15** and **D15**).

7. In cell **C6**, enter the formula =C5*$B$15. The **$** symbols fix this reference as *absolute*.

8. Copy the formula across the range **D6:E6** and observe the result. View the contents of **D6** and **E6** to check that all formulas use **B15** for the **VAT Rate**.

> **Note:**   You can also make only a column or row reference absolute. For example, **$B15** makes the column reference absolute; **B$15** makes the row reference absolute.

9. Complete the **Total Price** row by adding the **Price** and **VAT** for each month. Cell **F7** should contain the final overall total **£22,573.20**.

10. Save the workbook as **parts complete** and close it.

3.5 Linking Cells

In *Excel*, you can easily reference the contents of cells that exist on other worksheets. To do this, you simply create a formula which contains a **link** to the other worksheet's cells.

Linked cell references include the name of the source worksheet, then an **!** (exclamation mark) symbol, followed by a cell reference. For example, the formula **=Accounts!C10** links to the contents of **C10** on the **Accounts** worksheet.

> **Note:**   Importantly, if any updates are made to the source worksheet, these changes are automatically updated in the linked cell also.

Activity:

1. Open the workbook **Events** which features incomplete accounts for the park's *Demon of the Deep* ride. This workbook contains three worksheets. Click on each name tab to view their contents.

2. Return to the incomplete **Events** worksheet. Information for **Decorations**, **Promotions** and **Advertising** has not yet been entered.

3. Select cell **B7**. Rather than copy the information from the other worksheets, let's link to it instead. That way, any changes made at a later date will be automatically shown on the **Events** worksheet.

4. Start the formula by pressing =.

5. Next, click on the **Decorations** name tab and select the cell **B5** (the total cost for all decorations in *January*). Press <**Enter**>. The value **423** appears.

6. Select **B7** again and examine the contents of the **Formula Bar**. Notice that the cell is linked to **B5** on the **Decorations** worksheet.

7. The formula in cell **B7** now needs to be copied to the range **C7:M7**. Use the **Fill Handle** to do this now.

> **Note:**   The **Fill Handle** also automatically updates linked cells that use relative addressing.

8. Use the same technique to link the range **B8:M8** to the range **B5:M5** on the **Promotions** worksheet.

9. Experiment by changing values in the ranges **B2:M4** on both the **Decorations** and **Promotions** worksheets. Examine the impact of those changes on the **Events** worksheet.

10. Save the workbook as **events updated** and leave it open for the next exercise.

3.6 Linking Between Workbooks

As well as linking to cells on other worksheets, it is also possible to link to cells in other workbooks.

Cells linked in this way will include the name of the source workbook, the name of the source worksheet, then an **!** (exclamation mark) symbol, followed by a cell reference. For example, the formula **=[Budget.xlsx]Accounts!C10** links to the contents of **C10** on the **Accounts** worksheet in the **Budget** workbook.

> **Note:** Again, if any updates are made to the source worksheet, these changes are automatically updated in the linked cell also.

Activity:

1. Open the workbook **Advertising** and examine its contents. The information shown needs to be included in the **events updated** workbook.

2. Leave **Advertising** open and return to **events updated**.

3. Select cell **B9** and press **=** to start a formula.

4. Display the **Advertising** workbook again and select the cell **B5** (the total cost for all advertising in *January*). Press <**Enter**>.

5. You are automatically returned to the **events updated** workbook and the linked value **525** appears in cell **B9**. Select cell **B9** again and examine the contents of the **Formula Bar**. Notice that the cell is linked to **B5** on the **Costs** worksheet in the **Advertising** workbook.

> **Note:** By default, cell references across workbooks are made absolute. You can change this manually by removing the **$** symbols.

6. By editing the formula in the **Formula Bar**, change the *absolute* cell reference in **B9** to a *relative* cell reference. This will allow you to use the **Fill Handle** to copy the formula.

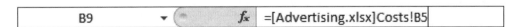

> **Note:** Press <**Enter**> on your keyboard or click the **Enter** button, ✔, on the **Formula Bar** to confirm changes. The **Cancel** button, ✕, can be used to abandon the change.

7. Now, use the **Fill Handle** to copy the formula in cell **B9** to the range **C9:M9**. As a relative cell reference is used in **B9**, *Excel* automatically updates the copied formulas.

8. Experiment by changing values in the range **B2:M4** on the **Advertising** worksheet. Examine the impact of those changes on the **Events** worksheet.

9. Save the **events updated** workbook and close it. Then, close the **Advertising** workbook <u>without</u> saving changes.

> **Note:** When you open a workbook that contains links to other workbooks, you are prompted to update the links and retrieve the latest data.

10. Open the workbook **events updated** again. A dialog box appears informing you that the workbook contains links to other data sources.

> **Note:** Depending on your computer's security settings, a yellow **Security Warning** banner may appear at the top of the screen. If this happens, select **Enable Content**. Then, save the workbook, close it and return to step **10** to continue.

11. Read the dialog box and then click **Update**. *Excel* silently opens the **Advertising** workbook, updates the contents of the linked cells, and then closes it again.

12. Save the **events updated** workbook again and close it.

3.7 Develop Your Skills

At the end of every section you will find a *Develop Your Skills* activity. Work through it to ensure you have fully understood the previous exercises and can demonstrate the practical skills learned.

1. Open the workbook **Components**. This spreadsheet shows the output from four local factories that are used to manufacture ride components for *Big Planet Theme Park*.

2. In cell **H5**, enter a simple formula to work out the total number of **Screws** produced across the four factories.

3. Use the **Fill Handle** to replicate the formula in **H5** down to **H8**. Check that relative cell addressing has updated the cell references correctly.

4. In cell **C10**, use a formula to calculate the total output of **Factory 1** for the month.

5. Use the **Fill Handle** to replicate the formula in **C10** across to **F10**. Check that relative cell addressing has updated the cell references correctly.

6. The component **Price** values, in the range **B5:B8**, are missing. However, they can be located on the **Prices** worksheet. Create a link to these cells.

7. Enter a formula in **I5** to calculate the total cost of **Screws** produced by all four factories.

8. Use the **Fill Handle** to replicate the formula in **I5** down to **I8**. Check that relative cell addressing has updated the cell references correctly.

9. The cost of components does not include VAT. Enter a formula in **J5** to work out the VAT payable on the value in cell **I5**.

> **Hint:** Multiply the total **Cost** of screws produced by all factories by the **VAT Rate** in **B12**.

10. Use the **Fill Handle** to replicate the formula in **J5** down to **J8**.

11. Are the copied formulas producing a result of **£0.00**? If so, you did not use an absolute cell reference to the VAT rate in **J5** – correct this now and copy the formula again.

12. The components produced by all four factories will be *divided up equally* and distributed to **10** repair teams around the park. Enter a formula in cell **H12** to work this out.

> **Hint:** You may need to use brackets to force the correct order of operations.

13. Copy the formula in **H12** to cells **I12** and **J12** (and apply the correct **Number Format**).

14. Finally, save the workbook as **components complete** and close it.

> **Note:** A model solution for this activity is provided in the **Sample Solutions** data folder.

3.8 Section Summary

Well done! You have now completed all of the exercises in *Section 3: Formulas*. Using the practical knowledge and skills learned you should now be able to:

- Create simple formulas to perform calculations

- Use mathematical operators such as add, subtract, multiply and divide

- Use brackets to force the order of a formula's operation

- Copy formulas to different cells

- Understand relative and absolute cell addressing

- Link cells across worksheets

- Link cells across workbooks

> **Note:** If you feel you are unsure about any of the topics covered in this section, you should revisit the appropriate exercises and try them again before moving on.

Section 4

Functions

By the end of this section you should be able to:

Understand Functions

Use Insert Function and AutoSum

Apply Mathematical Functions

Apply Statistical Functions

Apply Date and Time Functions

Apply Logical Functions

Apply Lookup Functions

4.1 Functions

Functions are small programs that are built into *Excel* to help save you time when creating a formula. There are various types of function available, but the following are used most often:

Date & Time	DATE, TIME, TODAY, NOW
Math & Trig	SUM, ROUND, ROUNDUP, ROUNDDOWN
Statistical	AVERAGE, MAX, MIN, COUNT, COUNTA, COUNTIF
Lookup & Reference	HLOOKUP, VLOOKUP
Logical	IF, AND, OR

Don't worry if you find the concept of functions a little confusing at the moment. For now, you simply need to understand that, when used, they can help create complex formulas quickly and easily.

> **Note:** All functions perform a specific task. The most popular type of function is **SUM**, which simply adds a range of cells together and *returns* the result.

Activity:

1. Open the workbook **Sum**. This spreadsheet contains four columns of identical numbers that you will now add together using different techniques.

2. Select cell **B13** and examine the contents of the **Formula Bar**. A formula is present in this cell that adds the contents of the range **B2:B11**.

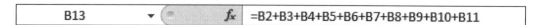

| B13 | ▼ | f_x | =B2+B3+B4+B5+B6+B7+B8+B9+B10+B11 |

> **Note:** Imagine if there were 100 numbers in this column, or 1000, or 10,000! It would take forever to create a formula to add them together.

3. The **SUM** function should be used instead to add large amounts of numbers. This function takes a range of cells as an *input* and returns the summed result as an *output* (i.e. the result of adding all of the cell contents together).

> **Note:** Think of a function as a little machine with an opening for inputs and an exit for outputs. You place items in one end (i.e. values or cell references), the machine does something with them, and then it returns the result.

4. Select cell **C13**. To add the numbers in the range **C2:C11**, type **=SUM(C2:C11)**. Notice the blue rectangle that appears on the sheet to mark the range used by the function.

> **Note:** It is very important that you enter the <u>exact</u> function name or it will not work. *Excel* will automatically convert lower case names to upper case for you.

	IF	▼	X ✓ fx	=SUM(C2:C11)	
	A	B	C	D	E
1					
2		1	1	1	1
3		2	2	2	2
4		3	3	3	3
5		4	4	4	4
6		5	5	5	5
7		6	6	6	6
8		7	7	7	7
9		8	8	8	8
10		9	9	9	9
11		10	10	10	10
12					
13	Total:	55	C2:C11)		

5. Press <**Enter**> to complete the function and see the result (which, as you would expect, is the same as cell **B13**).

> **Note:** It is very difficult to remember all of the functions built in to *Excel*. Luckily you don't need to – the **Insert Function** feature can be used instead.

6. Select cell **D13**. On the **Formula Bar**, click the **Insert Function** button.

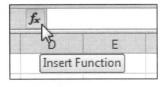

7. The **Insert Function** dialog box appears.

8.   From the "select a category" drop-down menu, select each category in turn to see all of the available functions – there are well over 200! In this exercise we will use **SUM**...

9.   Select the category **Math & Trig**. From the **Select a function** list, find and select the function **SUM**. Notice the brief description of the function that appears towards the bottom of the dialog box

> **SUM(number1,number2,...)**
> Adds all the numbers in a range of cells.

10.   Click **OK**. The **Function Arguments** dialog box is displayed, prompting for a range of numbers to send to the function.

11.   Click the **Collapse** button, [icon], to the right of the **Number1** box. This hides most of the dialog box and lets you select a range in the workbook by clicking and dragging.

12.   Click and drag the range **D2:D11**. The range appears in the collapsed dialog box.

8	8	8	8	
9	9	9	Function Arguments	
10	10	10	D2:D11	
55	55	D2:D11)		

13.   Click the **Expand** button, [icon], to restore the collapsed **Function Arguments** dialog box

14.   Click **OK**. The function is entered into the worksheet and the result displayed.

15.   Display the **Formulas** tab and explore the **Function Library** group. Notice the various functions available within each drop-down button.

16.   Save the workbook as **sum complete** and leave it open for the next exercise.

4.2 AutoSum

Formulas containing the **SUM** function are so popular that a specific button is available on the **Ribbon** to automatically create them.

Activity:

1. Using the workbook **sum complete**, select cell **E13**.

2. Next, display the **Home** tab and click the **Sum** button, $\boxed{\Sigma}$, in the **Editing** group. This feature is more popularly known as **AutoSum**.

> **Note:** **AutoSum** will automatically look up and down for numbers to sum first and then left to right. If the range it finds is wrong, simply click and drag to select a new one.

3. *Excel* automatically looks for nearby numbers to add. In this case the three cells to the left are found. Click and drag to select the range **E2:E11** instead.

SUM		✕ ✓ ƒx	=SUM(E2:E11)			
	A	B	C	D	E	F	G
1							
2		1	1	1	1		
3		2	2	2	2		
4		3	3	3	3		
5		4	4	4	4		
6		5	5	5	5		
7		6	6	6	6		
8		7	7	7	7		
9		8	8	8	8		
10		9	9	9	9		
11		10	10	10	10		
12							
13	Total:	55	55	55	=SUM(E2:E11)		
14					SUM(**number1**, [number2], ...)		

4. Press <**Enter**> to insert the function. That's all there is to it! Select cell **E13** again and notice that the formula **=SUM(E2:E11)** appears in the **Formula Bar** again.

> **Note:** *Excel* automatically updates ranges when columns/rows are inserted/deleted.

5. Insert a new row before row **5**. Enter the value **10** in <u>all</u> cells in the range **B5:E5**.

4		3	3	3	3
5		10	10	10	10
6		4	4	4	4

6. Notice the totals in the range **B14:E14**. The formulas which use the **SUM** function have been automatically updated to take into account the newly inserted row. The manual formula entered into **B14** has not.

> **Note:**   A useful way to check formula references is to double-click the required cell. The formula is displayed in the cell with colour coding to show which cells are used.

7. Double click cell **B14**. The cells used in the formula are highlighted on the worksheet. Notice that the new cell **B5** is not included.

SUM		✕ ✔ *fx*	=B2+B3+B4+B6+B7+B8+B9+B10+B11+B12			
	A	B	C	D	E	F	G
1							
2		1	1	1	1		
3		2	2	2	2		
4		3	3	3	3		
5		10	10	10	10		
6		4	4	4	4		
7		5	5	5	5		
8		6	6	6	6		
9		7	7	7	7		
10		8	8	8	8		
11		9	9	9	9		
12		10	10	10	10		
13							
14	Total:	=B2+B3+B4+B6+B7+B8+B9+B10+B11+B12					
15							

8. Press <**Esc**> to exit in-cell editing (or click the **Cancel** button, ✕, on the **Formula Bar**).

> **Note:**   Using ranges in your formulas helps to make sure that errors are not introduced into your spreadsheets when columns/rows are inserted/deleted.

9. Next, double-click cell **C14**. A single box shows the entire range used by the formula. Notice that *Excel* has automatically increased its size to include the newly inserted row.

> **Note:**   As you will see later, you can drag the range rectangle to another location in the worksheet and even click and drag its corners to expand or contract the selection.

10. Save the workbook using the same file name and close it.

4.3 Rounding

The range of mathematical functions includes three useful features for rounding decimal numbers. These are:

ROUND	rounds a number to a specified number of digits, up or down
ROUNDUP	always rounds a number *up* to a specified number of digits
ROUNDDOWN	always rounds a number *down* to a specified number of digits

Activity:

1. Open the workbook **Rounding**.

2. Select cell **C5**. On the **Formula Bar**, click the **Insert Function** button to display the **Insert Function** dialog box.

3. From the "select a category" drop-down menu, select the category **Math & Trig**. Then, from the **Select a function** list, find and select the function **ROUND**. Read the brief description of the function that appears and then click OK.

> **Note:** When rounding numbers, you can select the number of decimal places to round to.

4. In the **Number** box enter the cell reference **B5**. Then, in the **Num_digits** box, enter **2** to round the value to two decimal places. Click **OK** and observe the results.

5. With cell **C5** selected, examine the **Formula Bar**. Notice that the function **ROUND** is used with two *arguments*: the cell reference and the number of decimal places to round to.

C5   ▼   *fx*   =ROUND(B5,2)

6. Edit the formula to round up or down – whichever is nearest – to **0** decimal places instead: **=ROUND(B5,0)**. Then, copy the formula in cell **C5** to the range **C6:C22**.

7. Next, use the function **ROUNDUP** in cell **D5** to round up the contents of cell **B5** to **0** decimal places. Again, copy the formula to the range **D6:D22** and observe the result.

8. Then, use the function **ROUNDDOWN** in cell **E5** to round down the contents of cell **B5** to **0** decimal places. Copy the formula to the range **E6:E22** and observe the result.

Decimal	Round	Round Up	Round Down
0.473245556	0	1	0
0.539951706	1	1	0
1.083261469	1	2	1

9. Save the workbook as **rounding complete** and close it.

4.4 Statistical Functions

Statistical functions deal with analysing numbers, from simple counting of cells to useful calculations such as averages. The most popular statistical functions include:

COUNT	Counts cells that only have numbers in them
COUNTA	Counts cells with any content (text or numbers)
AVERAGE	Finds the mean average of a range of cells
MAX	Finds the largest number in the selected range
MIN	Finds the smallest number in the selected range
COUNTIF	Counts cells that contain numbers if they match a condition

Activity:

1. Open the worksheet **Numbers**.

2. How many numbers would you say there are in column **B**? To find out move to cell **A102** and type **Count:**.

3. Move to cell **B102** and click the **Insert Function** button, f_x. From the **Statistical** category, select **COUNT** and click **OK**.

> **Note:** Recall that *Excel* tries to automatically find cells to work with when using a function. If it gets things wrong, it is easy to enter the correct range manually.

4. Delete the contents of **Value1** and enter the range **B1:B100** instead. Click **OK**.

5. This result **99** is displayed; the number of cells in the range that contain numbers. Scroll up to find a missing number in the range (cell **B56**).

6. Enter **23** in the empty cell and press **<Enter>**. Scroll back down to the bottom of the list to see that cell **B102** now reads **100**.

7. In cell **A103** type **Average:**. Then, move to cell **B103** and click the **Insert Function** button again.

8. From the **Statistical** category, select **AVERAGE** and click **OK**.

9. Enter the range **B1:B100** again in the **Number1** box and click **OK**. This displays **50**, the average of the numbers in the specified range.

> **Note:** When the **Average** or **Count** functions are used, cells which are blank are ignored. However, cells containing zeros are included in the calculations.

10. Move back to the top of the worksheet and, in cell **D11**, type **Count:**.

11. Next, in cell **D12**, type **CountA:**.

12. In **E11**, use the **Count** function to count all of cells in the range **E1:E9**.

13. Similarly, in **E12**, use the **CountA** function to count all of the cells in the range **E1:E9**.

Count:	5
CountA:	8

> **Note:** The **COUNT** function only counts cells that contain numbers. However, the **COUNTA** function counts cells that contain both numbers and text.

14. In cell **A104** enter the text **Max:**. Move to **B104** and insert the function **MAX** from the **Statistical** group. Enter the range **B1:B100** and click **OK**. This gives the *maximum* value present in the specified range (**123**).

> **Note:** If you know a function's name, you can enter it manually into the **Formula Bar**.

15. In cell **A105** type **Min:** and in cell **B105** enter the formula **=MIN(B1:B100)**.

16. Press <**Enter**>. This gives the smallest value present in the specified range (**1**).

17. Finally, enter **Count If:** in cell **A106**. Then, insert the function **COUNTIF** in cell **B106**. Enter the range **B1:B100**.

> **Note:** The **COUNTIF** function will only count cells that match certain conditions (these conditions are known as **criteria**).

> **Note:** To specify function criteria in *Excel*, you can use the standard mathematical operators: less than (<), greater than (>), greater than or equal to (>=), less than or equal to (<=), and not equal to (<>).

18. In the **Criteria** box, enter **>50** and click **OK**. This gives the number of numeric cells present in the specified range which contain values that are greater than 50 (**48**).

101		
102	Count:	100
103	Average:	50
104	Max:	123
105	Min:	1
106	Count If:	48
107		

19. Change the contents of cell **B100** to **201**. Observe the effects on the results of all functions in the range **B102:B106**.

20. Save the workbook as **functions** and close it.

4.5 Date and Time Functions

There are a number of useful functions available in *Excel* for working with dates and times. The most popular include:

DATE	Inserts a specific date into a cell based on the arguments given
TIME	Inserts a specific time into a cell based on the arguments given
TODAY	Inserts the *current* date into a cell
NOW	Inserts the *current* date and time into a cell

It is important to understand that the date is stored within a cell as a simple number (e.g. 41020) that represents the number of days that have passed since January 1, 1900. By applying a **Number Format** of **Date** this can be formatted to appear in a more recognisable form (e.g. 21 April, 2012).

Similarly, time is stored within a cell as a decimal number between 0 and 1 (e.g. 0.5) that represents a fraction of a day. By applying a **Number Format** of **Time**, this can also be formatted to appear in a more recognisable form (e.g. 12:00:00).

> **Note:** Calculations are performed using the numbers which represent dates and times.

Activity:

1. Open the workbook **Order**. The first worksheet contains an incomplete purchase order form for ride components.

> **Note:** The keyboard shortcut <**Ctrl ;**> can be used to insert the current date into a cell.

2. Select cell **C4**. Using your keyboard, press <**Ctrl ;**> to insert the current *date*. Notice that it appears in the short form: DD/MM/YYYY. Press <**Enter**> to confirm the entry.

> **Note:** This date is **static** and will not change if the spreadsheet is opened on another day.

3. Select cell **C4** again. Then, using the **Number Format** drop-down button in the **Number** group, select **General**. This shows the date in its unformatted form (a simple number that represents the number of days that have passed since January 1, 1900).

4. Using the **Number Format** drop-down button in the **Number** group, select **Long Date**.

> **Note:** The keyboard shortcut <**Ctrl Shift ;**> can be used to insert the current time in a cell.

5. Next, select cell **C5**. Using your keyboard, press <**Ctrl Shift ;**> to insert the current *time*. Notice that it appears in the form: HH/MM. Press <**Enter**> to confirm the entry.

> **Note:** This time is also **static** and will never change.

6.   Select cell **C5** again.

> **Note:**   Notice that **Custom** is selected in the **Number Format** drop-down button. By default, the custom time format selected displays only hours and minutes.

7.   Using the **Number Format** drop-down button in the **Number** group, select **General**. This shows the time in its unformatted form (a decimal number between 0 and 1 that represents the current time as a fraction of a day).

8.   Then, use the **Number Format** button again to select **Time**. It now appears in the form HH:MM:SS.

Purchase Order

Date of Issue:	02 November 2012
Time of Issue:	13:36:00

> **Note:**   One number can be used to represent both a date *and* time. For example, 41020.5 represents 21/04/2012 12:00:00 (formatted using a **Number Format** of **Custom**).

9.   Next, display the **Report** worksheet. This contains a list of all components currently in stock.

10. Move to cell **C4** and click the **Insert Function** button. From the **Date & Time** category, select **TODAY** and click **OK**.

11. Read the dialog box that appears and then click **OK** again. Today's date appears in-cell and the formula **=TODAY()** appears in the **Formula Bar**.

12. Next, select cell **C5** and insert the function **NOW**. Today's date *and* time appears in-cell and the formula **=NOW()** appears in the **Formula Bar**.

13. Apply a **Number Format** of **Time** to cell **C5** to show only the current time.

> **Note:**   Cells using the functions **TODAY** and **NOW** are **dynamic** and will be automatically updated when the workbook is opened (or <F9> is pressed to update formulas).

14. Press <F9>. If the current time has changed, the value in **C5** changes to match.

> **Note:**   As dates and times are represented by numbers, it is easy to perform simple calculations based on them.

15. Select cell **C7** and enter the formula **=C4-C6** (the current **Report Date** minus the **Last Report** date). The number of days between those dates, **21**, appears.

> **Note:** The **DATE** function allows you to create a valid new date using three arguments: **Year**, **Month** and **Day**.

16. Notice that the range **E10:G13** contains information about the dates of previous orders. These would look better if formatted as a valid date.

17. Select cell **H10** and enter the formula **=DATE(E10,F10,G10)**. A new date is returned in the form DD/MM/YYYY.

18. Double-click cell **H10** to examine the cells used by the function. Then, press **<Esc>** to cancel in-cell editing.

19. Copy the formula in cell **H10** to the range **H11:H13**.

Current Stock Report

Report Date:	02/11/2012
Report Time:	14:10:55
Last Report:	12/10/2012
Days elapsed:	21

| | | | Date of Previous Order | | | |
Item ID	Description	Stock Level	Year	Month	Day	Previous Order
A10234	Screws	256	2012	1	31	31/01/2012
C20345	15cm Bolts	514	2012	6	23	23/06/2012
A10948	20cm Bolts	214	2012	5	7	07/05/2012
Z00123	Rivets	875	2012	10	29	29/10/2012

> **Note:** Notice the two-tiered use of column labels in the range **E8:G9**. This is a professional way to use headers and sub-headers in *Excel*.

20. As they no longer need to be shown, hide columns **E**, **F** and **G**.

> **Note:** The lesser used **TIME** function also allows you to create a new time using three arguments: **Hour**, **Minute** and **Second**.

21. Save the workbook as **order complete** and close it.

4.6 IF Functions

The widely used **IF** function checks a value or the contents of a cell and, if a **logical test** is passed, performs one action; if not, it performs another. The function takes the following form:

IF(*logical_test,value_if_true,value_if_false*)

> **Note:** The logical **IF** function is sometimes described as an **IF THEN ELSE** function: **IF** a condition is true **THEN** do this **ELSE** do that.

Activity:

1. Open the workbook **Bonus**. This spreadsheet contains the start of a simple calculation for working out sales bonuses.

2. In this example, staff at the park's *Gift Shop* get a bonus of **£100** if their weekly sales are over **£1,000**. Select cell **E6**.

> **Note:** Recall that many popular functions are also available in the **Function Library** on the **Formulas** tab.

3. Rather than using the **Insert Function** dialog box, try displaying the **Formulas** tab and clicking the **Logical** button in the **Function Library** group instead. From the options that appear, select **IF** to display the **Function Arguments** dialog box.

4. Read the description that appears in the lower half of the dialog box, and then enter the function arguments as shown below. Click **OK** and observe the result.

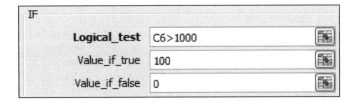

> **Note:** The function first performs the **Logical_test**, asking **IF** the value in **C6** is greater than **1000**. It is, and so it performs the **Value_if_true** part of the function and places the value **100** in the cell.

5. Change the value in **C6** to **£800** and press <**Enter**>. Observe the result.

> **Note:** As the sales are now under **1000**, the **Logical_test** fails and the **Value_if_false** part of the function is performed. In this case, the value **0** is placed in the cell.

6. Change the value in **C6** to **£2,500** and press <**Enter**>. The bonus is reapplied.

7.   Use the **Fill Handle** to copy the formula in **E6** to the range **E7:E10**.

Weekly Bonus Calculation				
			Wages	
Person	Sales	Basic	Bonus	Total
Bill	£2,500	£1,500	£100	£1,600
Emma	£1,300	£1,500	£100	£1,600
Jaz	£800	£1,500	£0	£1,500
Colm	£2,250	£1,500	£100	£1,600
Lisa	£900	£1,500	£0	£1,500
		£7,500	£300	£7,800

Note: You can also place **IF** functions *inside* other **IF** functions as **Value_if_true** or **Value_if_false** arguments. These are known as **Nested IF** functions and, although complicated at first glance, are in fact quite simple to use.

8.   Select cell **E6** and examine the formula in the **Formula Bar**. Park management has decided that if an employee makes more than **£2,000** in sales their bonus should be increased to **£200**. How can this be achieved?

9.   Let's replace the **Value_if_true** argument with a *second* **IF** function. Using the **Formula Bar**, change the **Value_if_true** argument as follows:

=IF(C6>1000,**IF(C6>2000,200,100)**,0)

10.   Press <**Enter**> and copy the new formula to the range **E7:E10**. Notice the effect.

Weekly Bonus Calculation				
			Wages	
Person	Sales	Basic	Bonus	Total
Bill	£2,500	£1,500	£200	£1,700
Emma	£1,300	£1,500	£100	£1,600
Jaz	£800	£1,500	£0	£1,500
Colm	£2,100	£1,500	£200	£1,700
Lisa	£900	£1,500	£0	£1,500
		£7,500	£500	£8,000

Note: The **IF** function first performs the first **Logical_test**. If this returns true the second **IF** is performed (outputting either **200** or **100**), otherwise **0** is placed in the cell.

11.   Save the workbook as **bonus complete** and close it.

4.7 AND Functions

Another useful logical function is the **AND** function. This performs two or more logical tests and, if _all_ are passed, it outputs **TRUE**. However, if even _one_ logical test fails, it outputs **FALSE**. The function takes the following form:

AND(_logical_test1,logical_test2,..._)

> **Note:**   Remember that the **AND** function can be used to perform two _or more_ logical tests.

Activity:

1.   Open the workbook **Visitors**. This spreadsheet contains visitor details for the theme park's _Laser Show_. For each of the four weeks described, notice that _target_ visitor numbers are also given (i.e. the number of visitors that the show is aiming to attract).

2.   Select cell **F5**. This cell should indicate whether all weekly targets have been achieved (i.e. each week's visitor numbers were greater than or equal to their target).

3.   Using whichever technique you prefer, insert the logical function **AND**. Read the brief description that appears at the bottom of the **Function Arguments** dialog box.

4.   Then, enter the function arguments as shown below.

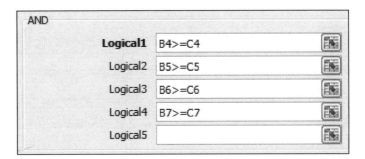

5.   Click **OK**. The value **FALSE** is placed in the cell, indicating that _at least one_ of the logical tests failed. Can you tell which?

6.   That's right – the visitor number in **B6** was less than its target. Change the amount in **B6** to **3100** and observe the result (all logical tests have now been passed).

7.   Next, change the value in **B7** to **1900**. This value is now less than its target and so fails the logical test. **FALSE** appears in cell **F5** again.

> **Note:**   You can use the **AND** function together with the **IF** function to build more complex logical tests.

8.   Delete the formula in cell **F5**.

9.   Then, using whichever technique you prefer, insert the logical function **IF**.

10. In the **Function Arguments** dialog box, enter the following **Logical_test**:

AND(B4>=C4,B5>=C5,B6>=C6,B7>=C7)

11. Enter **Yes** in the **Value_if_true** box and **No** in the **Value_if_false** box.

> **Note:**   Notice the quotation marks, **" "**, that appear around the text values **Yes** and **No**. These are *required* in any function where you wish to output text.

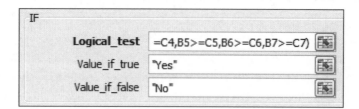

12. Click **OK** and, as you would expect, the text **No** appears in the cell. Examine the formula that appears in the **Formula Bar**.

> *fx*   =IF(AND(B4>=C4,B5>=C5,B6>=C6,B7>=C7),"Yes","No")

> **Note:**   It is the *output* of the **AND** function that is used in the **IF** function's logical test.

13. Change the value in cell **B7** to **3205** and the text **Yes** appears instead.

	A	B	C	D	E	F	G
1	Laser Show Visitors (Month 1)						
2							
3		Visitors	Target				
4	Week 1	2199	2000		Monthly targets achieved		
5	Week 2	3222	3000		*All:*	Yes	
6	Week 3	3100	3000		*At least one:*		
7	Week 4	3205	2000				
8							

> **Note:**   The **NOT** function can be used to test for the *reverse* of a condition. For example, **=NOT(B4>1000)** will return **FALSE** when **B4** is greater than **1000** (and vice-versa).

14. Save the workbook as **visitors updated** and leave it open for the next exercise.

4.8 OR Functions

Another logical function similar to **AND** is the **OR** function. This performs two or more logical tests and, if *at least one* is passed, it outputs **TRUE**. However, if *all* logical tests are failed, it outputs **FALSE**. The function takes the following form:

OR(*logical_test1,logical_test2,...*)

> **Note:** The **OR** function can be used to perform two *or more* logical tests.

Activity:

1.   Using the workbook **visitors updated** saved in the previous exercise, select cell **F6**. This cell should indicate whether *at least one* of the weekly targets has been achieved.

2.   Using whichever technique you prefer, insert the logical function **OR**. Read the brief description that appears at the bottom of the **Function Arguments** dialog box.

3.   Then, enter the function arguments as shown below.

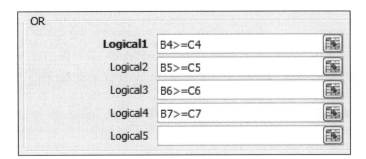

4.   Click **OK**. The value **TRUE** is placed in the cell, indicating that *at least one* of the logical tests passed.

> **Note:** You can also use the **OR** function together with the **IF** function to build more complex logical tests.

5.   Edit the formula in the **Formula Bar** so that the **OR** function appears as the logical test in a new **IF** function:

=IF(OR(B4>=C4,B5>=C5,B6>=C6,B7>=C7),"Yes","No")

> **Note:** Remember to use quotation marks around all text values in a function.

6.   Press <**Enter**> and, as you would expect, the text **Yes** appears in the cell.

7.   Experiment by changing the various visitor and target numbers and observe the effect on the **AND** and **OR** function outputs.

8.   Save the workbook using the same file name and close it.

4.9 Lookup Functions

Lookup functions are very useful tools for finding values in a **data table** (i.e. a range of cells containing information). The two most useful functions include:

HLOOKUP   Looks up a value in a horizontal (left to right) table
VLOOKUP   Looks up a value in a vertical (top to bottom) table

Using the following *horizontal* data table, for example, the **HLOOKUP** function will output a **10%** discount when looking up the value for **5** people, or **25%** when looking up the value for **20**.

Discount Table							
No in Party	1	5	10	20	30	50	100
Discount	0%	10%	15%	25%	40%	45%	50%

By default, *Excel* will also automatically find the *closest* match <u>below</u> the look up value (if no exact match is found). For example, the **HLOOKUP** function will output a **10%** discount if looking up the value for **6** people, or a **25%** discount if looking up the value for **29** people.

Activity:

1. Open the workbook **Discount**. Notice that the first worksheet features a *horizontal* "lookup" data table (**Discount Table**) in the range **C15:I16**.

2. Select cell **D8**. The discount to be placed in this cell depends on the **Number in Party** value (shown in cell **D4**).

3. Using whichever technique you prefer, insert the **Lookup & Reference** function **HLOOKUP**. Read the brief description that appears at the bottom of the **Function Arguments** dialog box, and then enter the function arguments as shown below.

> **Note:**   The **Lookup_value** is cell **D4** (**Number in Party**). The **Table_array** is **C15:I16** (the **Discount Table** range without the labels), and the **Row_index_num** is **2** (to output values from the second row of the table).

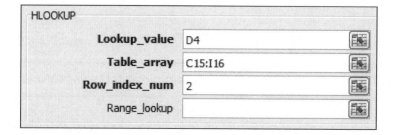

> **Note:**   Setting the **Range_lookup** to **FALSE** causes the function to output a value if and only if there is an <u>exact</u> match between the **Lookup_value** and the table entry. Leave it blank here.

4. Click **OK** and the value **10%** appears in cell **D8**. This produces a discount of **£9.98**. Examine the formula in the **Formula Bar**.

	A	B	C	D	E
1	**Park Entry Costs**				
2					
3		Entrance Fee		£19.95	
4		Number in Party		5	
5					
6		Total Price		**£99.75**	
7					
8		Discount %		10%	
9		Discount		£9.98	
10		Discount Price		**£89.78**	
11					

> **Note:** *Excel* searches for the value **5** in the first row of the lookup table. Once found, it then outputs its corresponding value in row 2.

5. Change the **Number in Party** value in **D4** to **23**. The **Discount %** changes along with the **Discount Price** producing a new discount of **£114.71**.

> **Note:** As there is not an exact value for **23** in the lookup table, *Excel* finds the closest match _below_.

6. Change the **Number in Party** value in **D4** to **55**. The **Discount %** changes to **45%** which is again reflected in the **Discount Price**.

> **Note:** Vertical lookups, using the **VLOOKUP** function, work in exactly the same way, but with data arranged vertically rather than horizontally.

7. Using the worksheet name tabs, display the **Vertical Lookup** spreadsheet. This is the same as the first worksheet but the **Discount Table** is now vertical.

8. Select cell **D8** and insert the **Lookup & Reference** function **VLOOKUP**. Then, enter the appropriate function arguments to create a suitable lookup.

D8	▼	*fx*	=VLOOKUP(D4,B16:C22,2)

9. Experiment by changing the various party numbers and observe the effect.

10. When you are finished, save the workbook as **discount updated** and close it.

4.10 Develop Your Skills

At the end of every section you will find a *Develop Your Skills* activity. Work through it to ensure you have fully understood the previous exercises and can demonstrate the practical skills learned.

1. Open the workbook **Analysis** which contains a spreadsheet of sales figures.

2. Using the **SUM** function, enter a formula in cell **B19** to calculate the **Total** of all sales in the *range* **B4:B17**.

3. Using the **AVERAGE** function, enter a formula in cell **B20** to calculate the **Average Sales**.

4. Next, use a function to find the **Number of Salespersons** and place the result in cell **B21**. Then, use a function to find the **Number of Sales Recorded** and place that result in **B22**.

> **Hint:** Recall the difference between **COUNT** and **COUNTA**.

5. Calculate the **Lowest Sales** and **Highest Sales** figures in cells **B23** and **B24**.

6. Count the **Number of Sales Over £1K** (i.e. >1000) and place that value in cell **B25**.

7. Select cell **C4**. The **+/- Average** is found by subtracting the **Average Sales** (cell **B20**) from an individual salesperson's **Sales**. Enter a simple formula to do this.

> **Hint:** You should use **Absolute** addressing for references to cell **B20**.

8. Using the **Fill Handle**, copy the formula down the column for all the other salespersons.

9. Two salespeople have no sales recorded. Does this affect the spreadsheet's results?

10. Enter **0** in cell **B8** and notice that the results of functions are now different. The average sales is lower and the lowest sale is now **0**. Enter **0** in cell **B13** too and observe the effect.

11. Use a function to place today's date in cell **G3** (in the format DD/MM/YYYY). Then, use another function to place the current time in cell **G5** (in the **Custom** format HH:MM).

12. In cell **G7**, use an **IF** function to display the text **Good sales!** if the value in **B19** is over **10,000** and **Bad sales!** if it is not.

13. Edit the formula so that **Good sales!** only appears if *both* the value in **B19** is over **10000** *and* the value in **B20** is over **1000**.

14. Use a **Lookup** function to work out each person's sales **Bonus** using the **Bonus Table**.

15. Save the workbook as **analysis complete** and close it.

> **Note:** A model solution for this activity is provided in the **Sample Solutions** data folder.

4.11 Section Summary

Well done! You have now completed all of the exercises in *Section 4: Functions*. Using the practical knowledge and skills learned you should now be able to:

- Understand, select and use a range of appropriate functions

- Apply statistical functions such as **COUNT**, **COUNTA**, **COUNTIF**, **AVERAGE**, **MIN** and **MAX**

- Apply mathematical functions such as **SUM**, **ROUND**, **ROUNDUP** and **ROUNDDOWN**

- Apply logical functions such as **IF**, **AND** and **OR**

- Apply date and time functions such as **DATE**, **TIME**, **TODAY** and **NOW**

- Apply lookup functions such as **HLOOKUP** and **VLOOKUP**

> **Note:** If you feel you are unsure about any of the topics covered in this section, you should revisit the appropriate exercises and try them again before moving on.

Section 5

Charts

By the end of this section you should be able to:

Identify and Create Different Chart Types

Move and Resize Charts

Move Charts to a New Worksheet

Understand Multiple Series

Plot Trends and Correlations

Format Charts

Add, Edit and Remove Labels

Customise Intervals and Scales

Select Data Sources

5.1 Creating Charts

Excel can take information stored in a worksheet and present it as an attractive chart. One important advantage of this is that the graphics created are much easier to understand at a glance. They can also be copied and pasted into other documents or presentations.

There are many different chart types available, each of which is generally best at displaying a specific type of information. The most popular and common chart types include:

Column	A very popular chart in *Excel*, this displays shaded vertical columns that represent values in different categories.	
Line	Specific values are plotted on the chart and are connected by a line. This is useful for displaying values that change over time.	
Pie	Values are shown as slices of a circular "pie", which highlights the contribution that each value makes to the total. Perhaps the simplest and most common of all *Excel* charts.	
Bar	Similar to a column chart, but the bars are shown horizontally.	
XY Scatter	Specific values are simply plotted on the chart. Different sets of values can have different plot symbols.	

> **Note:** It is important to understand that charts are dynamic. They will be automatically updated when the data that they reference is changed.

Activity:

1. Open the workbook **Survey**. This spreadsheet contains the results of a recent visitor survey conducted by *Fiona* at *Reception*. The number and type of participants can be seen in the range **A6:B9**.

2. *Fiona* is preparing a presentation and would like to display the results of her survey using a selection of simple charts. To begin with, she would like to create a pie chart which summarises the numbers and types of survey participants. Select the cell range **A5:B9**.

> **Note:** When selecting cells to turn into a chart, it is usually best to include row/column headers. *Excel* will automatically turn these into chart labels.

3. Display the **Insert** tab and examine the **Charts** group. Many popular charts can be created using the buttons shown here.

4. Click the **Pie** button and select the first type of 2-D chart in the list: **Pie** (a descriptive **ToolTip** will appear when you rest your mouse pointer over a chart type).

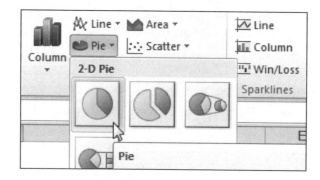

5. A chart is created from the selected data and each value is shown as a slice of the "pie".

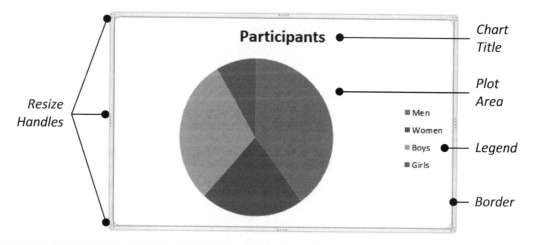

> **Note:** A **Chart Title** and colour-coded **Legend** is created based on the selected data labels.

6. Notice that the chart appears "floating" above the worksheet. Try moving it around by dragging the chart's **Border**, and then try scaling it using the **Resize Handles**.

7. With the pie chart selected, press <**Delete**> to remove it.

8. Display the **Insert** tab again and select **Bar**. Select the first type of 2-D bar in the list (**Clustered Bar**). A new chart is created that displays the selected data in a different way.

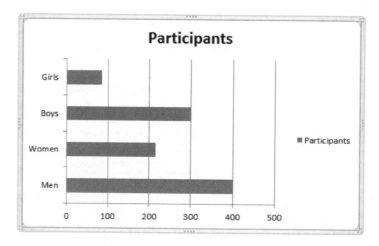

9. With the bar chart selected, press <Delete> to remove it.

10. To view all chart types available in *Excel*, click the **Other Charts**, 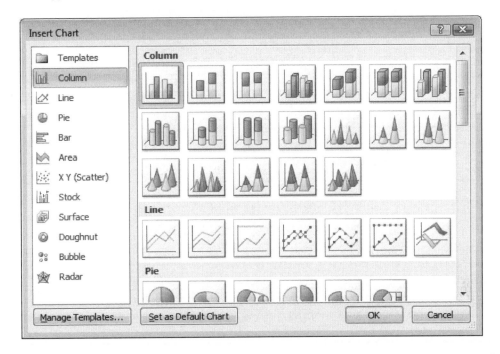, drop-down button in the **Charts** group (on the **Insert** tab). From the menu that appears, select **All Chart Types**. The **Insert Chart** dialog box appears.

11. Examine the types of charts that are available. The **Column** category is selected by default and the first type of column chart, **Clustered Column**, is selected (a **ToolTip** will again appear when you rest your mouse pointer over a chart type).

12. Click **OK** to create a chart of this type and examine the result. This is the same as a bar chart but the bars are shown as vertical columns instead.

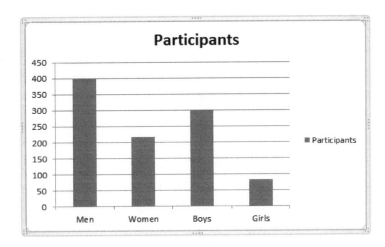

13. With the column chart selected, press <Delete> to remove it.

> **Note:** You will create more advanced chart types in the exercises that follow.

14. Save the workbook as **survey chart** and leave it open.

5.2 Multiple Series

In *Excel*, a **data series** is the name given to any range of cells that contain *related* values. As you have seen in the previous exercise, these can be selected and used to create a chart.

	Participants
Men	*399*
Women	*216*
Boys	*301*
Girls	*84*

> **Note:** In the above example, **Participants** is a data series with 4 related values. Likewise, **Men**, **Women**, **Boys** and **Girls** are all individual data series with 1 value each.

Each value in a data series is known as a **data point** and can be plotted on a chart. However, you can also create a chart based on more than one data series, allowing a direct comparison of values across different ranges.

Activity:

1. With the workbook **survey chart** open, select the range **A12:F16**.

> **Note:** Depending upon the chart you wish to create, the selected range contains either 5 data series (with four data points each) or 4 data series (with 5 data points each).

2. Using whichever technique you prefer, insert a simple 2-D **Clustered Column** chart.

> **Note:** Most chart types in *Excel* feature a horizontal **x** axis and a vertical **y** axis. These are used to measure, plot and categorize data points.

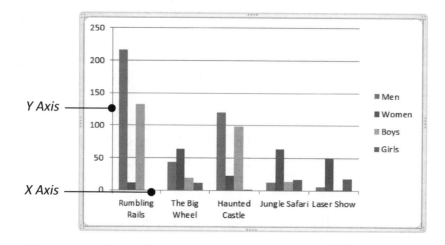

> **Note:** *Excel* automatically creates a chart with four data series: **Men**, **Women**, **Boys** and **Girls**. Each series is automatically given its own entry in the chart's **Legend**. Data points are grouped by ride type (x axis) and plotted against votes (y axis).

> **Note:** When a chart is selected three new **Chart Tools** tabs appear on the **Ribbon**. These can be used to customise your charts.

3. With the **Design** tab selected, click **Switch Row/Column** in the **Data** group to reverse the chosen data series and data points. Observe the effect.

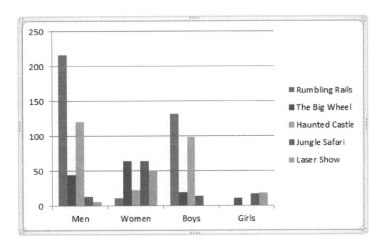

> **Note:** You should only group multiple data series if they share the *same scale*. For example, rainfall (cm) and sunshine (hours) use two very different scales and should therefore not be plotted on the same chart.

> **Note:** Once you have created a chart, you can change your mind and select another chart type instead.

4. In the **Type** group on the **Design** tab, click the **Change Chart Type** button.

5. Select **Bar** from the list of chart types available and then choose **Clustered Bar**. Click **OK** and observe the effect.

6. Use the **Switch Row/Column** button to reverse the data series and data points again.

> **Note:** If required, two or more non-adjacent data series (i.e. ranges that are <u>not</u> next to each other) can be selected by holding <**Ctrl**>.

7. Save the workbook using the same file name and close it.

5.3 Plotting Trends

Pie charts and bar/column charts are really useful for summarising data series and highlighting the differences between them. However, to better show how data series change over time (known as a **trend**), it is often best to use a **Line** chart instead.

Activity:

1. Open the workbook **Rainfall**. This spreadsheet contains two years worth of monthly rainfall measurements.

2. Select the range **A3:M5**. Then, using whichever technique you prefer, insert a simple 2-D **Line** chart. Notice that the data points for each of the two series are connected by a line.

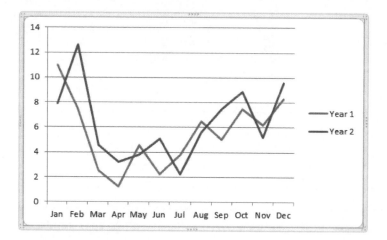

Note: *Excel* creates a chart with two data series: **Year 1** and **Year 2**. Data points are grouped by month (x axis) and plotted against rainfall amount (y axis).

3. To see the data points more clearly, markers can be used. In the **Type** group on the **Design** tab, click the **Change Chart Type** button.

4. Find and select the **Line** chart **Line with Markers**. Click **OK** and observe the effect.

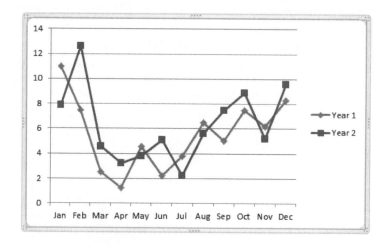

5. Save the workbook as **rainfall chart** and close it.

5.4 Correlations

A **Scatter** chart (or **scattergram**) can be used to show the relationship between two data series. More importantly, it can show how one data series affects – or is affected by – another.

> **Note:** The relationship between two data series is known as a **correlation**.

Activity:

1. Open the workbook **Repairs**. This spreadsheet shows the number of successful ride repairs completed during a recent ten week period.

2. Select the range **A3:K5**. Then, using whichever technique you prefer, insert a simple **Scatter with only Markers** chart.

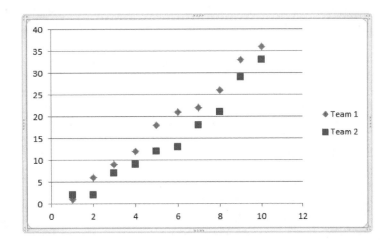

> **Note:** Notice that the data points for each of the two series are plotted on the chart as markers only (there are no connecting lines).

> **Note:** Charts are often used to make sense of a lot of information. As well as summarising data they can often highlight hidden trends and correlations.

3. What conclusion can you draw about the repair data from looking at the current chart?

4. The chart shows that, as time passes, the number of successful repairs increases. So, one can safely say that the longer a new repair team works together the better and more productive it becomes.

> **Note:** The chart shows a **positive correlation** between time (in weeks) and number of successful repairs. If repairs decreased over time, this would produce a **negative correlation** instead.

5. Save the workbook as **repairs chart** and close it.

5.5 Moving Charts

By default, *Excel* creates charts that are **embedded** on the same worksheet as your data. However, it is easy to move these charts to another worksheet.

Activity:

1. Open the workbook **Income**. This spreadsheet contains information on food, drink and gift sales at one of the theme park's restaurants. A **Line** chart with markers has already been created based on this data and appears in the centre of the worksheet.

> **Note:**   A chart can be cut (or copied) and pasted to another worksheet location.

2. Select the chart. Then, click the **Cut** button, ✂, in the **Clipboard** group on the **Home** tab (or press <**Ctrl+X**>). The chart is cut and placed on the **Clipboard** (in memory).

3. Create a new worksheet in the current workbook. Select cell **C5**.

> **Note:**   The top left corner of a pasted chart is placed in the currently selected cell.

4. Click the **Paste** button in the **Clipboard** group (or press <**Ctrl+V**>). The cut chart is pasted to the new location.

> **Note:**   A chart can be placed on its own full-screen worksheet (known as a **Chart Sheet**).

5. With the chart selected, display the **Design** tab and click the **Move Chart** button in the **Location** group.

Move Chart

6. Examine the **Move Chart** dialog box that appears.

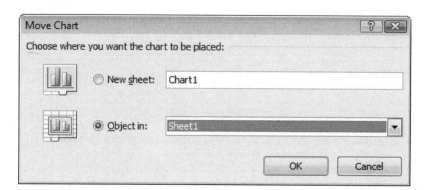

> **Note:**   The **Object in** box allows you to move the chart to an existing worksheet.

7. Select **New sheet** and enter **Line Chart** as its name.

8. Click **OK.** The chart is now displayed on a full-screen worksheet titled **Line Chart**.

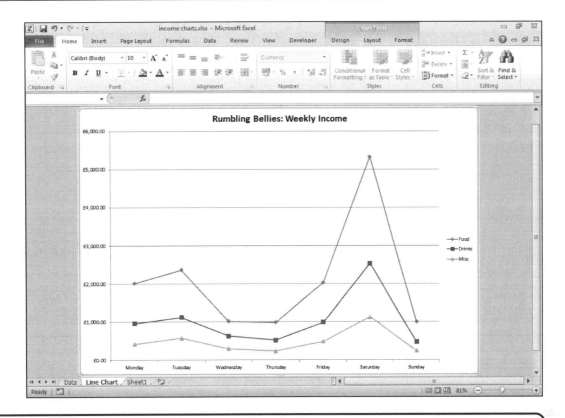

> **Note:** Recall that charts are dynamic. They will be automatically updated when the data they reference is changed.

9. Display the **Data** worksheet and select cell **D3**. Change this data label to **Gifts**.

10. Next, select cell **C7**. Change this value to **£2,500**.

11. Return to the **Line Chart** worksheet and observe the effect. Notice that the **Legend** and **Plot Area** have both been automatically updated.

12. Delete the empty **Sheet1** worksheet.

13. Then, save the workbook as **income charts** and close it.

5.6 Formatting Charts

Once *Excel* has created a chart for you, you can use the various **Chart Tools** features to change and customise its appearance.

> **Note:**   There are also many layouts, styles and effects that can be applied to charts. For example, different themed colours or an impressive 3D effect can be used.

Activity:

1.   Open the workbook **Charts**. This spreadsheet contains information from the *Pirate's Cove* that has been used to create three charts (each on its own worksheet).

2.   Display the **Pie Chart** worksheet and select the chart.

> **Note:**   All selected chart objects can be moved by clicking and dragging their borders.

3.   Click the **Legend** once to select it. Then, by dragging its border, move it to the left side of the chart.

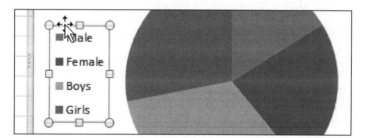

4.   Using the same technique, move the chart title (**Swimmers**) to the right of the chart.

> **Note:**   *Excel* features a number of built-in **Chart Layouts** that can be used to quickly rearrange chart objects with a single click.

5.   Locate the **Chart Layouts** group on the **Design** tab. Then, select the first item in the list to apply that layout style (a **ToolTip** displays the name **Layout 1**). Observe the effect.

— More

Chart Layouts

6.   Select each of the **Chart Layouts** styles in turn to see the various designs available. Additional styles can be found by clicking the **More** button.

> **Note:**   *Excel* also features a number of impressive built-in **Chart Styles**.

7. Locate the **Chart Styles** group on the **Design** tab. Select a variety of styles to automatically adjust the colours and visual appearance of the chart.

> **Note:**   More **Chart Styles** can be accessed by clicking the **More** button. Try some of the impressive 3D effects such as **Style 10** and **Style 26**.

8. When you are finished experimenting with different layouts and styles, choose **Layout 2** in **Chart Layouts** and **Style 10** in **Chart Styles**.

9. The chart already has a title but it is not very descriptive. Click the title **Swimmers** once to select it and then again to start editing. Change the title to **Pirate's Cove Swimmers**.

Pirate's Cove Swimmers

10. Click anywhere outside of the text box to confirm the change and deselect the chart's title.

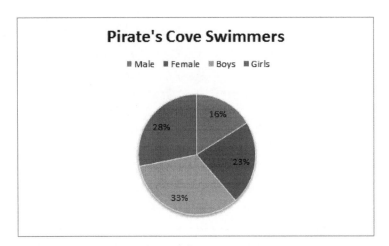

> **Note:**   Familiar font, border and background effects can also be applied to selected chart objects or to the chart as a whole.

11. Click an empty area of the chart to make sure the chart *as a whole* is selected (and not any of the individual chart objects such as the **Plot Area**, **Title** or **Legend**).

12. Display the **Format** tab and examine the various formatting that can be applied. Then, using the **Shape Fill** button in the **Shape Styles** group, apply a *light blue* background.

13. Similarly, use the **Shape Outline** button to apply a *dark blue* border with a **Weight** of **3 pt**.

> **Note:**   Once again, *Excel* features a number of impressive built-in **Shape Styles**.

14. Click the **More** button, ⬔, in the **Shape Styles** group. Examine the various styles available (place your mouse pointer over a style *without clicking* to preview it on the worksheet).

15. When you are finished previewing styles, select **Subtle Effect - Blue, Accent 1** (second from the left on the fourth row) to apply this preset border and background style.

16. Click once to select the chart's title label only. Then, using **Shape Styles**, apply the **Light 1 Outline, Colored Fill - Blue, Accent 1** (second from the left on the third row) to apply this preset border and background style to the *selected* chart object.

> **Note:** Standard font formatting features can also be used with chart and data labels.

17. Using the **Font** group on the **Home** tab, change the label's **Font Size** to **16** and the colour to dark blue.

18. Next, select the **Legend** and increase its **Font Size** to **12**.

> **Note:** More advanced formatting options can be accessed by right-clicking chart objects.

> **Note:** Used properly, formatting techniques can highlight important information and give your charts a more professional appearance. However, too many fancy fonts, styles and colours can often have the reverse effect.

> **Note:** If you are presenting your charts in print, be careful to choose colours that work well in black and white. *Excel* includes a number of **Pattern Fills** that can help.

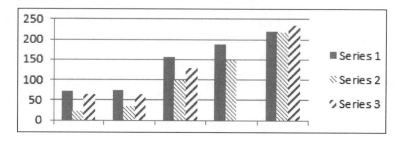

19. Save the workbook as **charts formatted** and leave it open for the next exercise.

5.7 Customising Labels

You can easily add, edit or remove useful data and axis labels that describe the contents and features of your chart.

Activity:

1. With the workbook **charts formatted** open, display the **Bar Chart** worksheet and select the chart. Display the **Layout** tab and examine the features available in the **Labels** group.

2. All good charts have a simple, meaningful title. To add one here, click **Chart Title**. From the menu that appears, select **Above Chart**. The series label **Swimmers** appears. Change this to **Pirate's Cove Swimmers** again.

3. The **Legend** is not very helpful here and can be removed. Select it and press <**Delete**>.

> **Note:** Notice that the chart's **Plot Area** is automatically resized when chart objects are added or removed.

4. Using the **Design** tab's **Chart Styles** options, select **Style 26** (second from the left on the fourth row) to apply an attractive 3-D effect to the **Plot Area**.

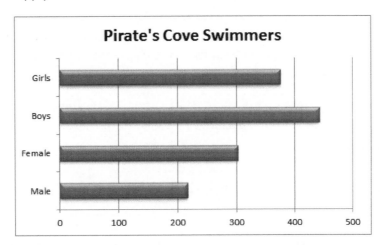

> **Note:** Useful **Data Labels** can be added to **Plot Area** items to display the exact values used to create them.

5. Display the **Layout** tab and click the **Data Labels** button. From the menu that appears, select **Center**. Data point values now appear in the centre of each bar.

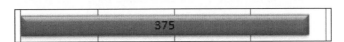

6. Click the **Data Labels** button again. From the menu that appears, select **Inside End**. Data point values now appear at the end of each bar.

7. Next, display the **Line Chart** worksheet and select the chart.

8.   Add the title **Pirate's Cove Facilities** above the chart.

9.   A chart with multiple series needs a **Legend** to explain what each item represents. Click **Legend** in the **Labels** group and select **Show Legend at Right**.

> **Note:**   A **Legend** (or **key**) is a chart object that identifies the patterns or colours assigned to each data series.

10. The values on the axes can also have labels attached which describe their scales. Click **Axis Titles** in the **Labels** group and select **Primary Horizontal Axis Title | Title Below Axis**.

11. A new label appears below the x axis. Change the text to **Days of the Week**.

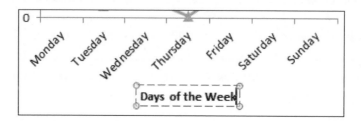

12. Next, click **Axis Titles** in the **Labels** group again. This time, select **Primary Vertical Axis Title | Rotated Title**. Change the new label's text to **Hours Used**.

> **Note:**   As well as a title, every chart should have two meaningful axis titles and, if applicable, a **Legend**. Without these the chart may not make sense to others.

13. Click an empty area of the chart. Then, using the **Format** tab's **Shape Styles** options, select **Subtle Effect - Blue, Accent 1** to apply this preset border and background style to the whole chart.

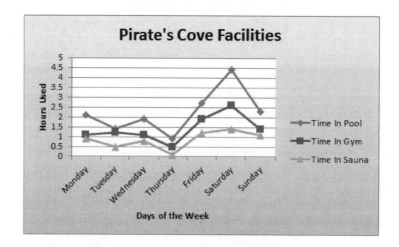

14. Save the workbook using the same file name and close it.

5.8 Intervals and Scales

To remove unnecessary empty space in a chart and focus on important data, you can adjust the **scales** on each axis (i.e. the *maximum* and *minimum* values shown). The intervals *between* the maximum and minimum values can also be changed.

Activity:

1. Open the workbook **Land Prices**. This spreadsheet features a **Line** chart which shows the cost of land purchased by *Big Planet Theme Park* over a ten year period.

2. Notice that the scale of the chart's y axis ranges from **0** to **100000**. However, there are no data points between **0** and **60000** or above **90000**.

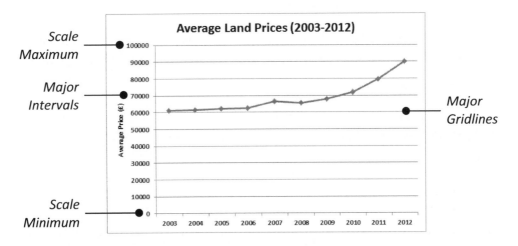

> **Note:** Notice also that the vertical axis's **intervals** increase by 10000 each time.

3. Click the chart to select it and then click the y-axis values once. Next, display the **Layout** tab and select **Format Selection** from the **Current Selection** group. The **Format Axis** dialog box appears.

> **Note:** You can also right-click an axis and select **Format Axis** (or double-click it).

4. Examine the **Axis Options** that appear. By default, *Excel* automatically selects the upper (**Maximum**) and lower (**Minimum**) bounds based on the data points in the chart.

5. Select the **Fixed** button for **Minimum** and change the value in the box to **60000**. Likewise, select the **Fixed** button for **Maximum** and change the value in the box to **90000**.

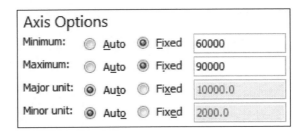

6. Click **Close**. The dialog box disappears and the chart is displayed with a more suitable scale. The changes in values over time are now much clearer.

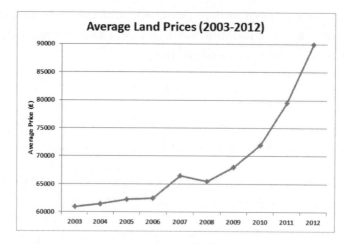

7. Notice that the **Major Intervals** between the maximum and minimum values have been automatically adjusted. With the y-axis values still selected, display the **Format Axis** dialog box again.

8. Select the **Fixed** button for **Major unit** and change the value in the box to **10000**. Similarly, select the **Fixed** button for **Minor unit** and change the value to **5000**.

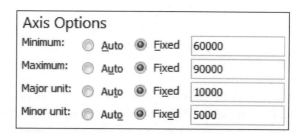

9. Click **Close**. The dialog box disappears and the chart is displayed with intervals of **10000**.

Note: **Major Intervals** are indicated on the **Plot Area** by horizontal **Major Gridlines**.

10. To view **Minor Gridlines**, display the **Layout** tab and click the **Gridlines** button in the **Axes** group. From the drop-down menu that appears, select **Primary Horizontal Gridlines | Minor Gridlines**.

Note: The techniques described in this exercise can also be applied to the horizontal axis.

11. Using the **Gridlines** button, select **Primary Vertical Gridlines | Major Gridlines**. Vertical gridlines now appear on the x axis.

12. Save the workbook as **land prices complete** and close it.

5.9 Selecting Data

When you create a chart you first select a range of cells to base it on. These references are known as the chart's **Data Source**. If at a later date you wish to change the **Data Source** (perhaps to include a new series of data), you can do so very easily.

> **Note:** *Excel* does not always get things right when it creates a chart. From time to time you may have to make manual changes to **Data Source** settings.

Activity:

1. Open the workbook **Profits** and examine the data that appears. Then, select the range **B4:C14** and insert a simple new 2-D **Clustered Column** chart.

2. Something has gone wrong. *Excel* has plotted both the **Year** and **Profits** data as two separate series which is incorrect (the **Year** column contains labels, not values).

3. With the new chart selected, display the **Design** tab and click the **Select Data** button in the **Data** group. The **Select Data Source** dialog box appears.

> **Note:** The **Chart data range** box can be used to select a completely new data series.

4. The data range selected is correct. However, the **Legend Entries** box incorrectly includes **Year** as a data series. Select this and click **Remove**.

5. Next, the **Horizontal (Category) Axis Labels** are incorrect. Click the **Edit** button.

6. When the **Axis Labels** dialog box appears, click and drag to select the range **B5:B14** on the worksheet (you can move the **Axis Labels** dialog box if it is in the way). Click **OK**.

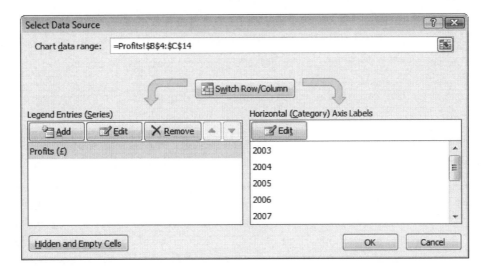

7. Click **OK** and observe the effect. The chart is now correct.

8. Save the workbook as **profits chart** and close it.

5.10 Choosing a Chart Type

There are over 70 different chart types available in *Excel* and choosing the right one can be tricky. However, your data and the information you wish to present will often limit your choice. For example, a data set containing a small number of related values may be best summarised using a **Pie** chart, but a large data set containing multiple series would not.

> **Note:** A chart's primary purpose is to present information to others. Before creating a chart, always try to consider your audience and think about your message. What is it that you are trying to say and which type of graph best helps you do this? Remember: a good chart should stand alone and require little explanation.

The diagram below suggests the most suitable chart styles for best presenting specific types of information. However, this should only be used as a guide – every situation is different and your choice of chart depends entirely on your data source and the message you want to get across.

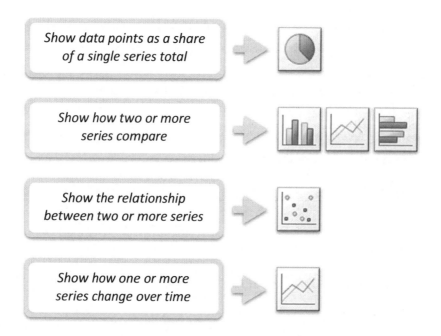

Of course, you can often take complex data and present summaries using simple, easy to understand charts. For example, the differences between data series with many data points is perhaps best presented as a **Column**, **Bar** or **Line** chart, but series totals or averages can quite easily be expressed as a **Pie** chart.

> **Note:** The *Big Planet Support* website contains a link to a handy resource that can help you choose the best chart type for a specific task. To find this, please visit **www.bigplanetsupport.co.uk** and navigate to **Useful Links > Course Support**.

5.11 Develop Your Skills

At the end of every section you will find a *Develop Your Skills* activity. Work through it to ensure you have fully understood the previous exercises and can demonstrate the practical skills learned.

1. Open the workbook **Sunshine**. This spreadsheet shows the data recorded by three sunshine detector stations at the park.

2. Create a simple **Pie** chart showing the number of breakdowns for all three stations.

> **Note:**   Remember to include row labels so that they appear in the chart's **Legend**.

3. Improve the visual impact of the chart by applying **Style 26** from **Chart Styles**.

4. Add the title **Station Breakdowns** *above* the chart and add **Data Labels** to the **Inside End** of the pie chart.

5. Move the chart to a *new* sheet and name it **Breakdowns**. Increase the **Font Size** for the *whole* chart to **20 pt**.

6. Return to the **Sunshine** worksheet and create a simple **Clustered Column** chart based on the range **A9:M10**. Remove the **Legend** and change the title to **Station A Sunshine**.

7. Add a **Primary Vertical Axis Title (Rotated Title)** and change the text to **Hours**.

8. Move the chart to a *new* sheet and name it **Station A**. Increase the **Font Size** for the *whole* chart to **20 pt**.

9. Return to the **Sunshine** worksheet and create a simple **Line** chart based on the range **A9:M11**. Add the title **Big Planet Sunshine**.

10. Add another **Primary Vertical Axis Title (Rotated Title)** and label it **Hours** again. Then, add a **Primary Horizontal Axis Title (Title Below Axis)** and label it **2012 Statistics**.

11. Format the **Y** axis and change **Minimum** to a **Fixed** value of **50** and **Maximum** to a **Fixed** value of **300**.

12. Edit the **Data Source** for the chart to include the data for **Station C**.

13. Move the chart to a *new* sheet and name it **All Stations**.

14. Increase the **Font Size** for the *whole* chart to **20 pt**. Then, change the colour of the **Chart Title** and **Axis Titles** to a dark blue colour.

15. Save the workbook as **sunshine complete** and close it.

> **Note:**   A model solution for this activity is provided in the **Sample Solutions** data folder.

5.12 Section Summary

Well done! You have now completed all of the exercises in *Section 5: Charts*. Using the practical knowledge and skills learned you should now be able to:

- Present information graphically

- Identify and create different chart types such as **Column**, **Line**, **Pie**, **Bar** and **XY Scatter**

- Choose the best chart type for your data

- Move and resize charts

- Move charts to a new worksheet

- Understand multiple series

- Plot trends and correlations

- Format charts

- Add, edit and remove labels such as title, axis and legend

- Customise intervals and scales

- Select and edit data sources

> **Note:**   If you feel you are unsure about any of the topics covered in this section, you should revisit the appropriate exercises and try them again before moving on.

Section 6

Working with Data

By the end of this section you should be able to:

Rearrange Data by Sorting

Reduce Data by Filtering

Use 'What-If' Analyses

Understand and Use Goal Seek

Model Outcomes

Understand and Use Scenarios

6.1 Tables

Although *Excel's* primary purpose is to record numbers and perform calculations, it is also frequently used to record simple **Tables** of data (also known as **Lists**). Similar in form to an *Access* database, each column in the table represents a single, separate piece of information. Entries in the table are then stored in rows known as a **records**.

	A	B	C	D	E	F	G
1				Survey Results			
2							
3	Surname	First Name	Sex	DOB	Age	Town	First Visit?
4	Poole	Janet	F	01/05/1998	14	Littletown	Yes
5	Robinson	Christopher	M	23/11/1985	26	Noplace	Yes
6	Allison	Brian	M	20/04/1962	50	Smallton	Yes
7	Robson	Barry	M	21/04/1966	46	Smallton	Yes
8	McKnight	Charles	M	05/03/1980	32	Noplace	
9	James	Peter	M	31/07/1997	15	Noplace	Yes
10	Frost	Marjorie	F	12/12/1987	24	Noplace	
11	Hooper	John	M	06/01/1999	13	Littletown	Yes
12	West	Gordon	M	23/11/1968	43	Littletown	
13	Luke	John	M	13/05/2003	9	Smallton	Yes
14	Curry	Basil	M	19/09/2002	10	Noplace	

Note: When creating a table in *Excel*, it is important that you enter the same type of information in each column.

As you will learn more about in this section, *Excel* features many useful and powerful tools for working with tables. In particular, it allows you to:

* Sort data alphabetically or numerically in ascending or descending order

* Search for matching criteria by filtering table entries

* Search or query a table to find specific data

* Perform statistical calculations on the data for analysis and to help with decision-making

Note: If a table becomes too large or complex, it should be noted that *Microsoft Access* is perhaps a more appropriate application to use.

Activity:

1.   Open the workbook **Research**. This spreadsheet contains the results of a recent visitor survey at the theme park.

2.   Examine the contents of the worksheet. It features a single table with 220 individual records. Notice the column header labels.

3.   Leave the workbook open for the next exercise.

6.2 Sorting Data

Sometimes you may need to **sort** the contents of a table so that related cells are grouped together or placed in a certain order. For example, you could rearrange the contents of a staff or product list alphabetically by name.

Activity:

1. Select any cell in column **A** that contains a **Surname** and, from the **Home** tab, click the **Sort & Filter** button in the **Editing** group. From the menu that appears, select **Sort A to Z**.

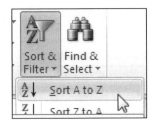

2. The records in the table are reordered alphabetically using the contents of column **A**.

	A	B	C	D	E	F	G
1				Survey Results			
2							
3	Surname	First Name	Sex	DOB	Age	Town	First Visit?
4	Ainslie	Ruth	F	28/05/1960	52	Noplace	Yes
5	Airey	Gordon	M	09/11/1964	48	Smallton	
6	Alberti	Franco	M	30/10/1969	43	Smallton	Yes
7	Alderson	Peggy	F	16/02/1957	55	Littletown	
8	Allison	Brian	M	20/04/1962	50	Smallton	Yes
9	Allott	Geoffrey	M	07/06/1934	78	Smallton	
10	Ambrose	Shiela	F	10/07/1966	46	Smallton	

> **Note:** *Excel* automatically detects and selects the whole table when sorting. Note also that entire records are sorted, not just the current column. However, if a range is selected first, only the contents of those cells will be sorted.

3. Select any cell in column **B** containing a **First Name** and, using the **Sort & Filter** button, select **Sort Z to A**. Records are sorted by **First Name** in *reverse* alphabetical order.

4. Select any cell in column **E** containing a number and click the **Sort & Filter** button. *Excel* recognises that the content of the selected cell is a number. Select **Sort Smallest to Largest** and the records are sorted by increasing **Age**.

5. Select any cell in column **D** containing a date and click the **Sort & Filter** button. Select **Sort Newest to Oldest** and the records are sorted by date of birth (**DOB**).

6. Using the same technique, sort the records **Oldest to Newest** by date of birth.

7. You can also create more complex, custom sorts. Select any *one* cell in the range **A4:G223** and display the **Data** tab. Examine the buttons in the **Sort & Filter** group.

> **Note:** Notice the buttons to perform **Sort A to Z**, $\begin{smallmatrix}A\\Z\end{smallmatrix}\downarrow$, and **Sort Z to A**, $\begin{smallmatrix}Z\\A\end{smallmatrix}\downarrow$. These are context sensitive and will perform different functions depending on the data type of the selected cells (i.e. **Sort Smallest to Largest** or **Sort Newest to Oldest**).

8. Click the **Sort** button to display the **Sort** dialog box. Select **Surname** from the **Sort by** drop-down box and make sure **A to Z** is selected in **Order**.

9. Click **Add Level**, ⌐_⌐ Add Level, to add another level to the sort. In **Then by**, select **First Name** and again make sure **A to Z** is selected in **Order**.

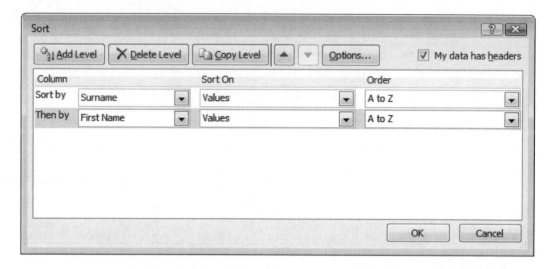

10. Click **OK** to apply the sort. The records are sorted on **Surname** and then on **First Name**.

148	Purvis	Lilly	F	14/07/1969	43	Noplace	
149	Rennison	Stuart	M	01/12/1953	58	Smallton	Yes
150	Richards	Mandy	F	15/11/1970	41	Littletown	
151	Ripon	Julia	F	18/09/1968	44	Noplace	
152	Roberts	Moira	F	13/10/1968	44	Littletown	
153	Robertson	Brian	M	13/02/1959	53	Noplace	
154	Robinson	Christopher	M	23/11/1985	26	Noplace	Yes
155	Robinson	Douglas	M	17/08/1918	94	Littletown	
156	Robinson	Harold	M	26/01/1949	63	Smallton	Yes
157	Robson	Barry	M	21/04/1966	46	Smallton	Yes
158	Rogers	Patrick	M	09/06/1966	46	Littletown	Yes
159	Rogers	Richard	M	15/09/1939	73	Littletown	
160	Rogers	Thomas	M	15/03/1987	25	Smallton	
161	Rose	Victor	M	18/05/1947	65	Littletown	
162	Royal	Susan	F	05/11/1968	44	Smallton	Yes
163	Sanderson	Peter	M	17/11/1945	66	Littletown	

> **Note:** It is now much easier to find information by visually scanning the data.

> **Note:** Sorting a table changes the order of rows permanently. Unlike filters, which you will learn more about in the next exercise, a sort cannot be turned off at a later time to restore the table's original order.

11. Save the workbook as **research sorted** and leave it open for the next exercise.

6.3 Filtering Data

Filtering is a simple technique for selecting records that match certain conditions (these conditions are known as **criteria**). Only the records that match the criteria are displayed; those that do not match are hidden. When a table is filtered, the worksheet is said to be in **Filter Mode**.

Activity:

1. Using the **research sorted** workbook, make sure the **Data** tab is displayed and any *one* cell in the range **A4:G223** is selected.

2. Select **Filter** from the **Sort & Filter** group. The worksheet enters **Filter Mode** and drop-down arrow buttons appear in the column headings in row **3**.

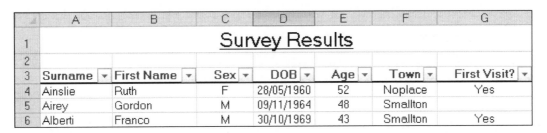

	Surname	First Name	Sex	DOB	Age	Town	First Visit?
	Survey Results						
4	Ainslie	Ruth	F	28/05/1960	52	Noplace	Yes
5	Airey	Gordon	M	09/11/1964	48	Smallton	
6	Alberti	Franco	M	30/10/1969	43	Smallton	Yes

> **Note:** The **Filter** tool automatically detects and selects the whole table. It also detects column header labels and then fills each drop-down filter list with all of the unique values that can be found in that column.

3. Click the **Town** drop-down filter arrow.

4. Then, deselect **Select All** and click to select **Littletown** instead.

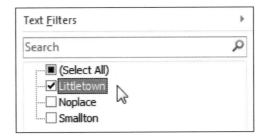

5. Click **OK** and only the people from **Littletown** are displayed in the worksheet.

> **Note:** The drop-down arrows gain a filter symbol, when the column is filtered.

6. Using the **Town** drop-down filter arrow again, click **Select All**.

7. Then, click **OK** to restore the table. All records reappear.

8. To display all the males from **Noplace** who were visiting the park for the first time, select only **M** from **Sex**, **Noplace** from **Town**, and **Yes** from **First Visit**.

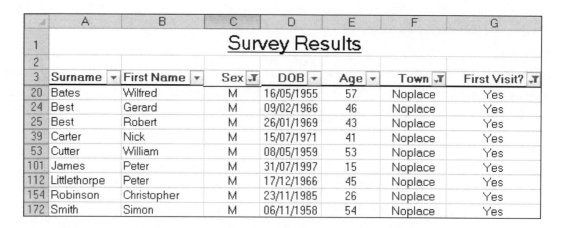

▲	A	B	C	D	E	F	G
1			Survey Results				
2							
3	Surname ▼	First Name ▼	Sex ⊤	DOB ▼	Age ▼	Town ⊤	First Visit? ⊤
20	Bates	Wilfred	M	16/05/1955	57	Noplace	Yes
24	Best	Gerard	M	09/02/1966	46	Noplace	Yes
25	Best	Robert	M	26/01/1969	43	Noplace	Yes
39	Carter	Nick	M	15/07/1971	41	Noplace	Yes
53	Cutter	William	M	08/05/1959	53	Noplace	Yes
101	James	Peter	M	31/07/1997	15	Noplace	Yes
112	Littlethorpe	Peter	M	17/12/1966	45	Noplace	Yes
154	Robinson	Christopher	M	23/11/1985	26	Noplace	Yes
172	Smith	Simon	M	06/11/1958	54	Noplace	Yes

> **Note:** The number of records found, **9 out of 220**, is shown on the **Status Bar**.

9. To redisplay the whole table again quickly, click the **Filter** button on the **Ribbon** to exit **Filter Mode**. The worksheet returns to its normal state.

> **Note:** You can also apply custom criteria for even more advanced filtering.

10. To only display the records of visitors who are less than 40 years old, enter **Filter Mode** again and select **Number Filters** from the **Age** drop-down list.

11. Examine the types of custom filters available. Then, select **Less Than** from the menu that appears and type **40** in the criteria box.

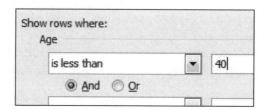

12. Click **OK** to filter the table. Only visitors less than 40 years old are now displayed.

13. To restore the table, drop-down the **Age** filter, click **Clear Filter From "Age"**.

14. Next, create a new filter to show only those people surveyed who are 40 years or older (i.e. greater than or equal to 40).

15. Restore the full table and then create another filter to show only those people whose **Surname** begins with **B**.

16. Restore the full table and then create a final filter to show only those people who were born between 01/04/1979 and 01/04/1989.

17. How many of the people found were visiting the park for the *first* time?

18. Save the workbook as **research filtered** and close it.

6.4 Advanced Filters

You can use standard logical operators and **wildcards** to help refine your filters and produce more precise results.

Activity:

1. Open the workbook **Bills**. A table appears containing invoices recently received by *Big Planet Theme Park's* construction department.

2. *Priti* from the construction team would like to find all records with invoice numbers that are *less than 200* <u>or</u> *more than 300*. Select any cell in the table and then click **Filter** from the **Sort & Filter** group to enter **Filter Mode**.

3. Next, click the **Invoice No.** drop-down filter arrow and expand **Number Filters**.

> **Note:** On the submenu that appears, *Excel* displays a selection of the most popular custom filters available. For more control, select **Custom Filter**.

4. Select **Custom Filter** to display the **Custom AutoFilter** dialog box. Complete the dialog box as shown below, making sure to select the **Or** logical operator.

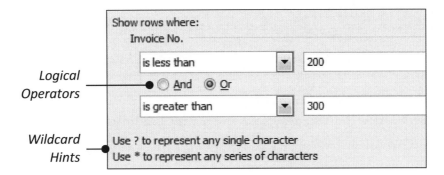

5. Click **OK** and examine the 12 records found. Then, click the **Clear** button in the **Sort & Filter** group to remove the filter and restore all records.

> **Note:** The built-in filters all produce a custom filter with the search criteria pre-selected.

6. Next, create a filter to only display records where the **Total** value is *greater than or equal to £600* <u>and</u> *less than or equal to £1,200*. 7 records are found.

7. Click the **Clear** button in the **Sort & Filter** group to remove the filter.

8. Now, create a new filter to display records where the **Company** text *begins with* the criteria **greens**.

9. Examine the 5 records found. Then, click the **Clear** button to remove the filter.

> **Note:** Wildcards are special symbols that can be used to select records containing values which are *similar* but not *exactly* the same as the search criteria. The most useful is the asterisk, *****, which can be used in place of one or more characters in a query.

10. To refine the previous search, create a new filter to display records where the **Company** text *equals* the following criteria: **greens * office**.

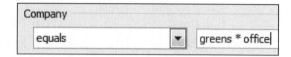

11. Click **OK**. 3 records are found where the **Company** text starts with **greens**, ends with **office**, and has any number of other characters in between.

> **Note:** For more control, the **?** wildcard symbol can be used in place of a *single* character.

12. Click the **Clear** button in the **Sort & Filter** group to remove the filter.

13. Then, create a new filter to display records where the **Company** text *begins with* the following criteria: **j?nes**.

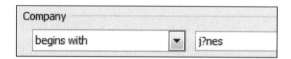

14. Click **OK** and examine the 6 records that are found. Due to the wildcard **?** symbol, records are selected where the **Company** text starts with **j**, is followed by any other single character, and then ends with **nes**.

15. Click the **Clear** button in the **Sort & Filter** group to remove the filter.

16. Try creating filters that show the following records:

    Bills where the **Invoice No.** is *between* **200** *and* **220** (10 records).

    Bills where the **Date** is *after* **15/12/2012** (14 records)

    Bills where the **Co. No.** (Company Number) is **134** *or* **345** (8 records)

    Bills where the **Company** name *ends with* the text **Sons** (7 records)

    Bills where the **Company** name *contains* the text **Joinery** (5 records)

    Bills where the **Company** name *begins with* **ja** and *ends with* **Joinery** (4 records)

    Bills where the **Total** value is *less than* **1000** *or more than* **2000** (21 records)

17. Save the workbook as **bills filtered** and close it.

6.5 Goal Seek

Goal Seek helps you to "model" real-life situations and find answers to "**What-If**" questions such as "*What price do I charge to make a profit?*" or "*How many items do I need to sell to break even?*". To do this, the tool automatically finds the best values to use in a formula to achieve a known, desired result.

Activity:

1. Open the workbook **Strike**. This spreadsheet shows the trading figures for a company that supplies cleaning products to the theme park.

2. Unfortunately there was a strike at the company last month. Change the **Sales** value in **C4** to **0**, the **Pay** value in **C8** to **0**, and the **Materials** value in **C10** to **0**.

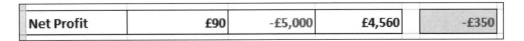

> **Note:** The company is now making a *total* loss of **£350** for all three months (cell **F16**).

3. It is important that the company breaks even (i.e. has a total **Net Profit** of 0). To do this, the **Price** that the company charges for its services *this month* could be increased.

> **Note:** The value in **D5** can be changed manually and the effects observed.

4. Change the value in **D5** to **£7.00** and press <**Enter**>. The total **Net Profit** is now **£2,350**. However, it is unlikely customers will be happy with such a large price increase.

5. Change the value in **D5** to **£6.10** and press <**Enter**>. The company makes a loss again.

> **Note:** You could keep altering the value in **D5** until the **Net Profit** is **0** (break even). However, this trial and error approach is haphazard and can take a lot of time.

6. To quickly find the lowest price needed to break even, the **Goal Seek** tool can be used. Click on cell **F17**, display the **Data** tab and click **What-If-Analysis** in the **Data Tools** group.

7. From the drop-down menu that appears, select **Goal Seek**. The **Goal Seek** dialog box appears with **F17** selected in the **Set cell** box.

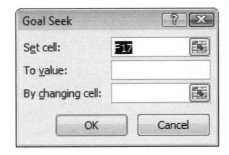

> **Note:** The **Goal Seek** dialog box is used to specify a cell to change to obtain (seek) a specific result (the goal).

8. Enter **0** in the **To value** box and **D5** in the **By changing cell** box. Click **OK** and the **Goal Seek** tool attempts to find a solution to the problem.

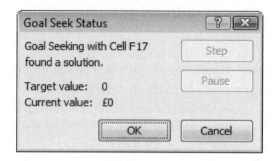

9. An exact solution is found and the worksheet updated. Notice that, by changing the value in cell **D5** to **£6.13**, the value **£0** is now obtained in cell **F17**.

> **Note:** If *Excel* finds more than one possible solution, you can step through them using the **Step** button.

10. Click **OK** to accept the change (**Cancel** will dismiss the changes and restore the original cell values). So, if the company raises this month's prices to **£6.17** it will break even.

	A	B	C	D	E	F
1	**Scrubbers Inc.**					
2				Forecast		
3		September	October	This Month		Total
4	Sales	2500	0	4500		7000
5	Price	£6.00	£6.00	£6.13		
6	Turnover	£15,000	£0	£27,583		£27,583
7	Workers	20	20	20		
8	Pay	£150	£0	£150		
9	Wages	£3,000	£0	£3,000		£6,000
10	Materials	£6,850	£0	£11,400		£18,250
11	Overheads	£5,000	£5,000	£5,000		£15,000
12	Spending	£14,850	£5,000	£19,400		£39,250
13	Profit	£150	-£5,000	£8,183		£3,333
14	Tax Rate	40%	40%	40%		120%
15	Tax	£60	£0	£3,273		£3,333
16						
17	Net Profit	£90	-£5,000	£4,910		£0

11. The company would still like to make a small profit. Use the **Goal Seek** tool to investigate how much the price in **D5** should be to produce a total **Net Profit** of **£100** in cell **F17**.

12. Save the workbook as **strike updated** and close it.

6.6 Scenarios

Excel's **Scenarios** tool is a simple feature that allows you to explore the outcomes of multiple "**What-If**" questions. To do this, a range of values is selected that represents a specific scenario (e.g. a best case scenario). More scenarios are then created that feature different cell values (e.g. the most likely or worse cases). You can then select each scenario at a time and see the impact that their different values have on the worksheet.

Activity:

1. Open the workbook **Forecast**. This spreadsheet has been created by *John* at the *IT Centre* to explore his department's budget for next year.

2. *John* has entered the money that he expects to spend on new IT purchases in the table (**B3:C14**). Unfortunately he has spent way too much, leaving the total budget (**F3**) overdrawn by **£13,000** (**F4**).

3. *John* would now like to create a number of different **Scenarios** to explore where savings can be made. Select the range **C4:C14**.

4. Using the **Data** tab, click the **What-If-Analysis** button. From the menu that appears, select **Scenario Manager**.

5. To start creating a new scenario, click **Add**. Enter the **Scenario** name as **Worst Case** and leave the **Changing cells** values as selected (**C4:C14**).

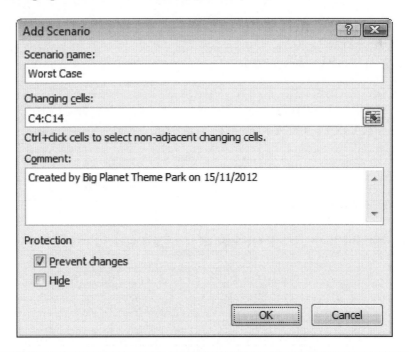

> **Note:**   Notice that you can enter a **Comment** to describe this **Scenario**.

6. Click **OK**. All of the values for the selected range are now shown. As this is probably the worst case scenario, leave the values as they are and click **OK** again.

7.   The new scenario **Worst Case** is now displayed in the **Scenarios** list.

8.   Let's create a new scenario to explore possible solutions to the problem. Click **Add**, enter the name as **Most Likely Case** and click **OK**.

9.   *John* does not have the money to upgrade everyone's computer next year. Change the values for **PCs** to **£9,000**, **Laptops** to **£6000**, and **Tablets** to **£5000**

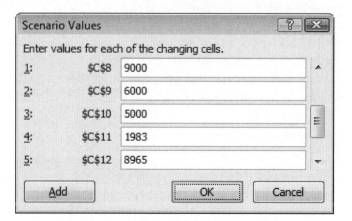

> **Note:**   Use the absolute references shown to the left of each value to identify cells.

10.   Click **OK**.

11.   Now, with the **Most Likely Case** scenario selected, click the **Show** button. The values on the worksheet are changed to those recorded for the **Most Likely** scenario. Notice that the **Remaining** figure in **F4** is now **£835** – within budget!

> **Note:**   The **Scenario Manager** dialog box can be moved to view cells underneath.

12.   *John* thinks he can make more savings. Add a new **Scenario** called **Best Case**, make sure the range **C4:C14** is still selected, and click **OK**.

13.   Using recycled printer cartridges, the cost of **Printer Ink** cost can be reduced to **£200**. Similarly, **Website** costs can be reduced to **£4,500**. Make both of these changes in the **Scenario Values** dialog box.

14.   Click **OK**. There are now three **Scenarios** in the list.

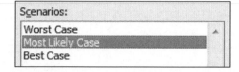

15.   Select each **Scenario** in turn and click **Show** to see the effect of applying each one.

16.   Finally, **Show** the **Most Likely Case** and then close the **Scenario Manager** dialog box.

17.   Save the workbook as **forecast scenarios** and close it.

6.7 Develop Your Skills

At the end of every section you will find a *Develop Your Skills* activity. Work through it to ensure you have fully understood the previous exercises and can demonstrate the practical skills learned.

1. Open the workbook **Temps**. This spreadsheet contains a list of temporary staff that have worked at the theme park in the past year.

2. Sort the staff members by **First Name (A to Z)**.

3. Next, create a custom sort that sorts by **First Name (A to Z)** and then by **Surname (A to Z)**.

4. Filter the employees to show only those who are *between* **20** *and* **30** years old (4 records).

5. **Clear** the filter.

6. Next, create another filter to show only those people whose **Payroll Number** is below **901240** *or* above **901250** (8 records).

7. **Clear** the filter.

8. Using a wildcard, create a custom filter to find people whose **Surname** begins with the letters **Ch** and ends with the letter **r** (2 records).

9. Display the **Hours** worksheet (using the worksheet name tabs). This spreadsheet contains the details of the hours worked by temporary staff.

10. Column **C** details the number of hours that temporary staff are scheduled to work next month. Unfortunately, the **Total Cost (C16)** exceeds the available budget (**B19**).

11. Create a new **Scenario** based on the current values in the range **C5:C14**. Name it **Over Budget** and close the **Scenario Manager**.

12. Perhaps the number of hours for **Week 10** (55) can be reduced? Use **Goal Seek** to find the best value to place in this cell so that the **Total Cost** is on budget (**£2,500**).

13. Create a second **Scenario** based on the current values in the range **C5:C14**. Name it **On Budget**.

14. Create a third **Scenario** named **Under Budget**. Enter values for **Week 3** as **20**, **Week 5** as **25**, and **Week 8** and **30**.

15. Show each of the Scenarios in turn and observe the effect on the worksheet.

16. Save the workbook as **temps complete** and close it.

> **Note:**   A model solution for this activity is provided in the **Sample Solutions** data folder.

6.8 Section Summary

Well done! You have now completed all of the exercises in *Section 6: Working with Data*. Using the practical knowledge and skills learned you should now be able to:

- Analyse and manipulate data stored in tables/lists

- Rearrange data by sorting

- Reduce data by filtering

- Perform advanced filters using logical operators and wildcards

- Perform "What-If" analyses to model real-life situations

- Understand and use goal seek

- Understand and use scenarios to model different outcomes

> **Note:** If you feel you are unsure about any of the topics covered in this section, you should revisit the appropriate exercises and try them again before moving on.

Section 7

Page Layout

By the end of this section you should be able to:

Print Worksheets

Use Print Preview

Set a Print Area

Change Page Layout Settings

Create and Edit Headers and Footers

Freeze Rows and Columns

7.1 Page Setup

Excel has a number of page setup features that let you modify how a worksheet will look when printed. You can adjust page **size**, **orientation**, **scaling** and **margins**.

Activity:

1.   Open the workbook **Turnover** which contains a breakdown of spending and net profits for special events at the *Haunted Castle*.

2.   Display the **File** tab and click **Print**. A preview of the first page as it will be printed is shown on the right.

3.   The worksheet stretches over two pages. Use the **Next Page** and **Previous Page** buttons at the bottom of the preview to move between pages.

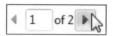

4.   With page 1 selected, click the **Portrait Orientation** drop-down button under **Settings**.

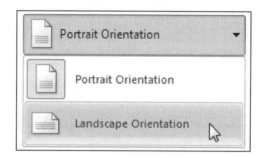

5.   Select **Landscape Orientation** from the drop-down menu and the page is rotated 90 degrees (although the contents of the workbook are not).

> **Note:**   The worksheet still covers two pages. To fit it onto one, there are two options available: **scale** the worksheet or reduce the page **margins**.

6.   Click the **No Scaling** drop-down button under **Settings** and select **Fit Sheet on One Page**.

7.   The worksheet is scaled down a little so that it fits onto one page. Select **No Scaling** from to return the worksheet to its original size.

8.   Next, click the **Custom Margins** (or similar) drop-down button. Examine the various margin settings that are available.

9.   Select **Narrow**. The margins are reduced and the worksheet again fits onto one page.

> **Note:**   The default paper size in all *Microsoft Office* applications is A4. However, it is possible to print on a variety of different paper sizes.

10. Click the **A4** drop-down button under **Settings** to see a list of the most popular paper sizes available.

11. Select **A5** (which is half the size of A4) and observe the effect. The worksheet now occupies two pages of A5 paper.

12. Restore the paper size to **A4** again.

13. By default, the **Heading Bars** and **Gridlines** between cells are not displayed when printed. However, this is easy to change. Click **Page Setup** (found at the bottom of **Settings**) to display the **Page Setup** dialog box.

14. On the **Sheet** tab, select both **Gridlines** and **Row and column headings**. Click **OK** and observe the effect.

15. Select an appropriate printer from the **Printer** drop-down box.

> **Note:** In some situations you may have access to more than one printer. Try to select and use the one closest to you. Remember: you may be charged for printing.

16. Make sure **Copies** is set to **1** to print a single copy of the current worksheet.

17. Click the large **Print** button to print to your chosen printer. You will be automatically returned to the main worksheet view.

> **Note:** Alternatively, click the **Home** tab to return *without* printing.

18. Display the **Page Layout** tab. Notice that, in the **Page Setup** group, the settings changed in this exercise can also be accessed from here.

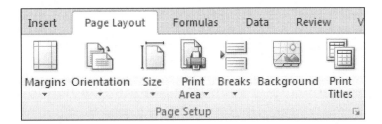

> **Note:** The disadvantage of making changes using this tab is that a preview is not shown.

19. Save the workbook as **turnover print ready** and close it.

7.2 Print Area

A **print area** can be set to only print a specific part of a worksheet. This range of cells will then be printed every time **Print** is selected.

Activity:

1. Open the workbook **Discount** and make sure the **Horizontal Lookup** worksheet is displayed. When printed, the **Discount Table** is not necessary and so should be left out.

2. Display the **Page Layout** tab and select the range **A1:D10**.

3. Click the **Print Area** button in the **Page Setup** ground and then select **Set Print Area**.

4. Click an empty cell outside of the selected range. Notice that a dotted line has appeared on the worksheet surrounding the range **A1:D10**. This is the **print area** and indicates the boundaries of the cell range that will be printed.

5. Display the **Print** screen and observe the effect. Only the selected range appears in the preview.

6. Click **Page Layout** to return to the worksheet without printing.

7. To remove the selected print area, click the **Print Area** button again and then select **Clear Print Area**.

> **Note:** Dotted lines may still appear on your worksheet that temporarily indicate the edge of the paper when printed (i.e. the default print area).

8. Save the workbook as **discount print ready** and leave it open for the next exercise.

7.3 Headers and Footers

Headers and **footers** are lines of text at the top and bottom of every printed page. As with *Microsoft Word*, you can insert automatic **fields** such as page number, date and time.

Activity:

1.   The workbook **discount print ready** should still be open. Display the **Insert** tab and click the **Header & Footer** button in the **Text** group.

2.   The header and footer areas appear on the worksheet. Examine the various useful options that appear on the **Design** tab.

> **Note:**   Editing headers and footers automatically changes the worksheet view to **Page Layout**. In this view, rulers appear towards the top and left edges of the worksheet. Any margins, headers or footers can also be seen.

3.   With the cursor flashing in the header's centre text box, enter the text **Park Entry Costs**.

4.   Click once in the left text box to move the cursor. Then, click **Current Date** in the **Header & Footer Elements** group.

5.   The text **&[Date]** appears in the text box. This is known as a **field code** and is updated automatically whenever your worksheet is opened or changed.

6.   Click once in the right-most header text box to move the cursor. Notice that the automatic field code in the leftmost box changes to the current date.

7.   In the **Navigation** group, click **Go to Footer**. In the left text box, type your own name.

8.   Move to the centre text box and click the **Sheet Name** button in the **Header & Footer Elements** group to insert the current worksheet's name. The field code **&[Tab]** appears.

> **Note:**   If you change the worksheet's name, the field code **&[Tab]** will be updated too.

9.   Move to the right text box to see the result of the field code.

10. Click the **Page Number** button to insert another automatic field. The field code **&[Page]** appears. Click away from the text box to see the effect.

11. Display the **View** tab and click **Normal** in **Workbook Views**. The margins and header/footer are hidden.

12. Display the **Print** screen and examine the print preview on the right. Notice the headers and footers and the updated field codes.

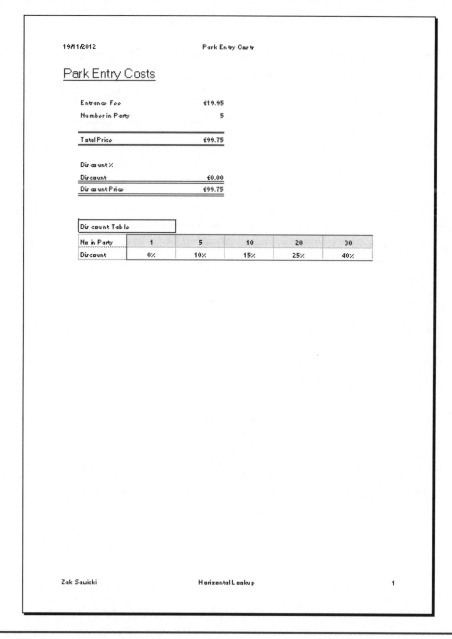

> **Note:** Similar header and footer settings can also be accessed from the **Print** screen's **Page Setup** dialog box (**Header/Footer** tab).

> **Note:** Standard font formatting can also be applied to headers and footers.

13. Save the workbook using the same file name and close it.

7.4 Freezing Cells

If you want to keep particular information on screen at all times (e.g. column and row header labels), you can **freeze** them in place. When scrolling through the data in a worksheet, the frozen cells will not move. An area that has been frozen in this way is known as a **Freeze Pane**.

Activity:

1.   Open the workbook **turnover print ready** that was saved earlier in this section.

2.   Display the **View** tab and click the **Freeze Panes** button in the **Window** group.

3.   From the drop-down menu that appears, select **Freeze Top Row**.

4.   The entire top row of the worksheet has now been frozen. Scroll down the worksheet and notice that the top row remains on-screen at all times (a horizontal line marks the **Freeze Pane** boundary).

5.   Click the **Freeze Panes** button again and select **Freeze First Column**. Scroll right and notice that the first column now remains on-screen at all times.

6.   Click the **Freeze Panes** button and select **Unfreeze Panes**. The frozen row and column are released.

> **Note:**   The **Freeze Panes** option on the **Freeze Panes** drop-down button can be used to freeze an entire area of a workbook above the active cell's row and to the left of the active cell's column.

7.   Select cell **B5**.

8.   Then, click the **Freeze Panes** button and select **Freeze Panes**. Notice that solid lines again mark the **Freeze Pane** boundaries.

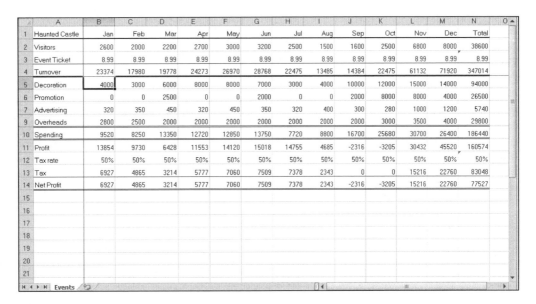

	A	B	C	D	E	F	G	H	I	J	K	L	M	N	O
1	Haunted Castle	Jan	Feb	Mar	Apr	May	Jun	Jul	Aug	Sep	Oct	Nov	Dec	Total	
2	Visitors	2600	2000	2200	2700	3000	3200	2500	1500	1600	2500	6800	8000	38600	
3	Event Ticket	8.99	8.99	8.99	8.99	8.99	8.99	8.99	8.99	8.99	8.99	8.99	8.99	8.99	
4	Turnover	23374	17980	19778	24273	26970	28768	22475	13485	14384	22475	61132	71920	347014	
5	Decoration	4000	3000	6000	8000	8000	7000	3000	4000	10000	12000	15000	14000	94000	
6	Promotion	0	0	2500	0	0	2000	0	0	2000	8000	8000	4000	26500	
7	Advertising	320	350	450	320	450	350	320	400	300	280	1000	1200	5740	
9	Overheads	2800	2500	2000	2000	2000	2000	2000	2000	2000	3000	3500	4000	29800	
10	Spending	9520	8250	13350	12720	12850	13750	7720	8800	16700	25680	30700	26400	186440	
11	Profit	13854	9730	6428	11553	14120	15018	14755	4685	-2316	-3205	30432	45520	160574	
12	Tax rate	50%	50%	50%	50%	50%	50%	50%	50%	50%	50%	50%	50%	50%	
13	Tax	6927	4865	3214	5777	7060	7509	7378	2343	0	0	15216	22760	83048	
14	Net Profit	6927	4865	3214	5777	7060	7509	7378	2343	-2316	-3205	15216	22760	77527	
15															
16															
17															
18															
19															
20															
21															

Events

9.   Scroll horizontally and vertically and observe the effect.

10. Click the **Freeze Panes** button and select **Unfreeze Panes**. The frozen pane is released.

11. Finally, experiment with **Freeze Panes** by creating and then releasing areas of the worksheet.

12. Save the workbook using the same file name and close it.

7.5 Develop Your Skills

At the end of every section you will find a *Develop Your Skills* activity. Work through it to ensure you have fully understood the previous exercises and can demonstrate the practical skills learned.

1. Open the workbook **Accounts**.

2. Insert a header and footer.

3. In the leftmost *header* text box, enter the label **Big Planet Accounts**. In the rightmost box, enter the **Current Date** using a field code.

4. In the centre of the *footer* area, use the **Header & Footer Elements** to create the following combination of text and field codes:

5. Click away from the footer text boxes to observe the result. Then, return to **Normal** view and preview how the worksheet will look when printed.

6. Check that **A4** is the selected page size, and then change the orientation of the page to landscape.

7. If necessary, scale the worksheet so that it fits on a single page.

8. Print a copy of the worksheet (or return to the **Home** tab without printing).

9. Set a print area that contains only the cell range **A1:D16**. Preview how the worksheet looks when printed.

10. Clear the print area.

11. Insert the following label in the empty centre textbox of the header: **First Quarter**. Make this text bold and italic.

12. Return to **Normal** view.

13. Freeze both the first row _and_ first column. Scroll horizontally and vertically and observe the effect.

14. Save the workbook as **accounts complete** and close it.

> **Note:**   A model solution for this activity is provided in the **Sample Solutions** data folder.

7.6 Section Summary

Well done! You have now completed all of the exercises in *Section 7: Page Layout*. Using the practical knowledge and skills learned you should now be able to:

- Print worksheets

- Use print preview

- Set a print area

- Change page layout settings (e.g. orientation, paper size, margins, scaling)

- Create and edit headers and footers

- Use field codes (e.g. date, sheet name, page number)

- Freeze rows and columns

> **Note:**   If you feel you are unsure about any of the topics covered in this section, you should revisit the appropriate exercises and try them again before moving on.

Section 8

Macros

By the end of this section you should be able to:

Understand Macros

Record a New Macro

Run a Macro

Assign Macros to Toolbar Buttons

Program a New Macro

Edit Macros

Delete Macros

Print Macros

8.1 Creating a Macro

Macros are small computer programs that can be used to perform a *custom* task in *Excel*. They simply contain a step-by-step list of cell selections and commands that, when "run", will be carried out in sequence. They are really useful for automating routine, everyday tasks.

> **Note:**   Macros are usually created by recording your actions as you perform a task. You can then play these actions back again – exactly as recorded – whenever needed.

Activity:

1.   Start a new, blank workbook. You will now create a macro to insert the theme park's address into the current worksheet.

2.   Display the **View** tab and click the **Macros** drop-down button (not the button's icon). From the menu that appears, select **Record Macro**.

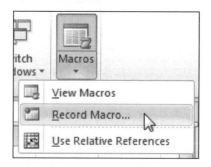

3.   The **Record Macro** dialog box appears. Overwrite the contents of the **Macro name** box with the text: **InsertAddress** (without spaces; spaces are not allowed in macro names).

4.   You can create a keyboard shortcut to run a macro. In the **Shortcut key** box, type the *lowercase* character **i**. You will be able to run this macro by pressing <**Ctrl i**>.

5.   In the **Description** box, enter the following: **A macro to insert and format my address**.

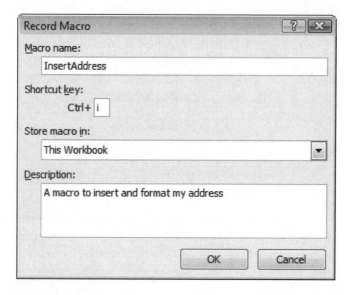

> **Note:** Be careful when defining keyboard shortcuts for macros. If the chosen key combination is already used for another function, your macro will take precedence.

6.   Click **OK**. All of the actions you now perform will be recorded. Select cell **B2** and enter **Big Planet Theme Park**. Press <**Enter**>.

7.   Next, enter **Learnersville** in cell **B3** and press <**Enter**>. Finally, enter the postcode **LV1 1BP** into cell **B4** and press <**Enter**>.

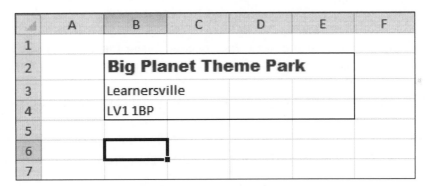

8.   Select cell **B2** again. Display the **Home** tab and use the formatting features in the **Font** group to make the selected cell's contents bold, dark blue and size **12**. From the **Font** drop-down, find and select the font type **Arial Black**.

9.   Select the range **B2:E4** and apply a single black outside border. Then select cell **B6**.

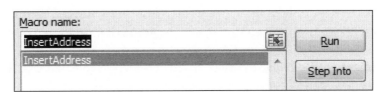

10. To stop recording, display the **View** tab and click the **Macros** drop-down button again. From the options that appear, select **Stop Recording**.

11. The macro is now complete. Using the worksheet name tabs, display **Sheet2**.

12. To run the new macro, click the **Macros** drop-down button again and select **View Macros**. The **Macro** dialog box appears.

> **Note:** Clicking the **Macros** button's icon will also display the **Macro** dialog box.

13. The new **InsertAddress** macro appears selected in the list. Notice the text that appears in the **Description** area at the bottom of the dialog box.

14. With the **InsertAddress** macro selected, click **Run**. The **Macro** dialog box is closed and the macro runs. All of the steps recorded are quickly performed again.

> **Note:** Only actions are recorded when creating a macro – the time you take is ignored. So, it pays to carefully consider your actions before performing them.

15. Display worksheet **Sheet3**. Press the keyboard shortcut **<Ctrl i>** to run the macro again.

> **Note:** By default, macros are recorded using absolute cell references. However, it is easy to use relative cell references instead.

16. Click the **Macros** drop-down button again. From the menu that appears, click to select **Use Relative References** (otherwise the macro will use absolute cell referencing).

17. Display the **Macros** drop-down button again. Then, select **Record Macro**.

Toggle Selected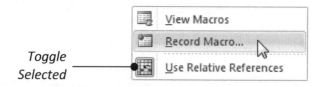

18. Give the new macro the name **InsertName**. Leave the **Shortcut key** option empty and enter the following text in the **Description** box: **A macro to insert and format my name**.

19. Click **OK**. In the currently active cell, enter your first name and press **<Enter>**.

20. Select the cell containing your name again and format the text to be italic, dark blue, size **22** and font type **Freestyle Script**. Centre the text horizontally and vertically in the cell.

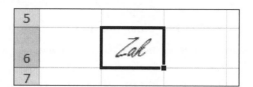

21. Display the **View** tab and click the **Macros** drop-down button again. From the options that appear, select **Stop Recording**. The new macro is now complete.

22. Create a new worksheet using the **Insert Worksheet** button. Then, select any cell and run the new macro **InsertName**. The macro inserts your formatted name.

23. Experiment with running the two macros created in this exercise. Observe the effect of using relative and absolute addresses.

24. Leave the workbook open for the next exercise.

8.2 Saving Macro-Enabled Workbooks

To save a workbook containing a macro it must be saved in a special **macro-enabled** file format.

> **Note:** As a macro is a small computer program, it is possible that spreadsheets sent or downloaded via the Internet can contain viruses. Always be careful when **enabling content** in *Microsoft Office* files from untrusted sources.

Activity:

1. Using the workbook created in the previous exercise, display the **Save As** dialog box.

2. Change the **File name** to **macros** and click **Save**. A message appears informing you that *Excel* is unable to save the workbook.

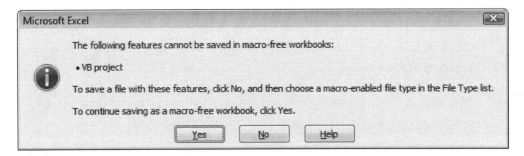

3. Read the contents of the dialog box and then click **No**. Then, expand the **Save as type** drop-down box and select **Excel Macro-Enabled Workbook**.

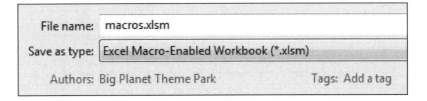

4. Notice that the new file will have a **.xlsm** extension instead of the normal **.xlsx**. Click **Save**.

5. Close the workbook and then try opening it again. A **Security Warning** appears in a banner below the **Ribbon**.

> **Note:** If you do not see the **Security Warning** banner and you are unable to run macros, click **File | Options | Trust Center | Trust Center Settings**. Then, select **Macro Settings** on the left and choose to **Disable all macros with notification**.

6. Until macros are enabled you will not be able to run them. Click **Enable Content**.

7. Leave the workbook open for the next exercise.

8.3 Assigning a Macro

To access and run macros faster, you can add shortcut buttons to the **Quick Access Toolbar**.

Activity:

1. Using the **macros** workbook, locate and click the drop-down arrow to the right of the **Quick Access Toolbar**.

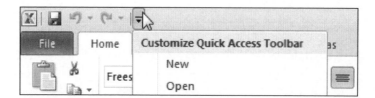

2. From the options shown, select **More Commands**. The **Excel Options** dialog box appears with options to **Customize the Quick Access Toolbar**.

3. Select **Macros** from the **Choose commands from** box. The two macros created earlier appear in the list below.

4. Click once on **InsertName** to select it. Then, click the **Add** button to add the macro to the **Quick Access Toolbar**. It now appears in the list on the right.

> **Note:** The position of buttons on the **Quick Access Toolbar** can be changed using the **Move Up** and **Move Down** arrows on the right.

5. With the macro selected in the rightmost list, click the **Modify** button below. You can choose an icon for the new toolbar button from those shown.

6. Select any icon that will help identify the purpose of the macro. Then, change the **Display name** to **Insert My Name** and click **OK** and **OK** again. The macro appears on the **Quick Access Toolbar**.

7. Select any empty cell and test the new toolbar button.

> **Note:** You can now run this macro in any workbook you like. However, *Excel* will need to open the **macros** workbook first (which it will do automatically).

8. Right click the new button and select **Remove from Quick Access Toolbar**.

9. Then, save the workbook using the same file name and close it.

8.4 Understanding the Code

All macros are created in a programming language called *Visual Basic*. When you record a macro, *Excel* automatically converts each action into a sequence of **commands**. This sequence is called programming **code** and can be edited or created from scratch.

> **Note:** You are not expected to be able to program a macro from scratch at this level. However, it is useful to see how a macro works by looking at its programming code.

Activity:

1. Open the workbook **Simple**. This spreadsheet contains a very simple macro that inserts two numbers into the current worksheet, a label, and a formula.

2. Firstly, click **Enable Content** if prompted to do so in order to allow macros to run.

3. Display the **View** tab and click the **Macros** button to display the **Macro** dialog box (or click the drop-down button and select **View Macros**).

4. Notice that there is already a macro recorded and selected. Click the **Run** button and observe the effect on the worksheet.

A simple calculation:		
		10
		20
Total:		30

5. To view the macro's code, display the **Macro** dialog box again and, with **SimpleCalculation** selected, click the **Edit** button.

6. A new *Visual Basic* editor window opens. Examine the contents of the main window which shows the macro's code (don't worry if it looks too complex at first glance).

```
Sub SimpleCalculation()
    '
    ' This is a simple macro created by Zak at
    ' Big Planet Theme Park
    '
    Range("B3").Value = "10"
    Range("B4").Value = "20"
    Range("A5").Value = "Total:"
    Range("B5").Formula = "=B3+B4"
End Sub
```

Macro Name — Sub SimpleCalculation()

Comments — ' Big Planet Theme Park

Commands — Range("B3").Value = "10"

> **Note:** Lines with an apostrophe character (') at the start are **comments** and are ignored when the macro is run. However, they are useful for describing a macro's purpose.

> **Note:** The macro starts with **Sub** which is short for **subroutine** (a small program), followed by the macro's name. **End Sub** marks the end of the macro's code.

7. By carefully editing the macro's code, make the following changes:

```
Sub SimpleCalculation()
'
' This is a simple macro created by Zak at
' Big Planet Theme Park
'
' This formula multiplies the values of B3 and B4
' and places the result in B5
'
    Range("B3").Value = "50"
    Range("B4").Value = "99"
    Range("A5").Value = "Total:"
    Range("B5").Formula = "=B3*B4"
End Sub
```

> **Note:** Notice that new comment lines have been added which describe the purpose of the function, and the values and formula used have been changed slightly.

> **Note:** If an error message appears you have made a mistake. Simply find and correct it.

8. Macro changes are saved automatically. Click the **Close** button, X, to return to *Excel*.

9. Run the macro **SimpleCalculation** again and observe the results.

> **Note:** For advanced users, a brand new macro can be programmed from scratch.

10. Display the **Macro** dialog box again. In **Macro** name, change the text to **HelloWorld** and click **Create**. A new, empty macro called **HelloWorld** appears in the editor window.

11. Create the new macro as shown below:

```
Sub HelloWorld()
' A macro to say hello to the world
    Range("D2").Value = "Hello World!"
End Sub
```

12. Well done. You have successfully created a brand new macro. Close the editor window and run it. The text **Hello World!** appears in cell **D2**.

> **Note:** As a macro is a computer program, you could say that writing one from scratch makes you a computer programmer. Well done!

13. Save the workbook as **simple macros** and leave it open for the next exercise.

8.5 Printing and Deleting Macros

Macros can easily be printed for reference or deleted. Once deleted, you can then save your workbook as a normal *Excel* file.

Activity:

1. Using the workbook **simple macros**, display the **Macro** dialog box.

2. Select **SimpleCalculation** and click **Edit**. To print this macro, select **File | Print** from the **Menu Bar**.

Note: You have the option to print the currently selected macro (**Current Module**) or all macros in the workbook (**Current Project**).

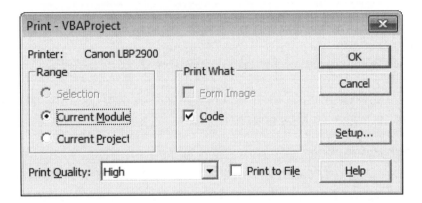

3. Under **Range**, select **Current Project** and click **OK**. All macros are printed.

Note: Alternatively, click **Cancel** to return to the editor without printing.

4. Close the editor to return to *Excel*. Display the **Macro** dialog box again.

5. Macros can easily be removed from a workbook. With the **HelloWorld** macro selected, click **Delete**.

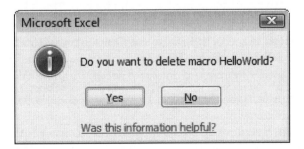

6. Click **Yes** and the macro will be deleted. Delete the macro **SimpleCalculation** as well.

7. Save the workbook as a normal **Excel Workbook** (using the **Save as type** drop-down on the **Save As** dialog box) with the name **simple without macros**. Then, close it.

8.6 Develop Your Skills

At the end of every section you will find a *Develop Your Skills* activity. Work through it to ensure you have fully understood the previous exercises and can demonstrate the practical skills learned.

1. Open the workbook **Football** (and **Enable Content** if prompted). This spreadsheet contains results from the *Big Planet Theme Park's* football league. Enter your name in **L3**.

2. The workbook already contains a macro. It sets a print area, prints the league table in **Landscape Orientation** (on your default printer), and then clears the print area. Run the macro and observe the results.

3. Edit the macro and increase the print area to include the **Points Table** (i.e. **A1:L13**).

> **Hint:** Change the code on line 6 to reference the range **$A$1:$L$13** instead.

4. Insert a new comment line *after* line 4 that reads: **Updated to include points table**.

5. Close the editor window and test the new macro.

6. Next, start recording a new macro named **SortLeague**. Enter the description: **This macro sorts the league table by points**.

7. Select any cell in the range **A3:I8**. Then, perform the steps needed to sort the league table by the number of **Points** (column **I**) *and then* on the **Goal Diff** (column **H**).

> **Hint:** Use the **Sort** button on the **Data** tab to create the sort shown below.

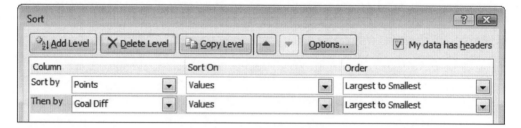

8. The *Construction* team are at the top of the league. Stop recording the macro.

9. Assign the macro to a new button on the **Quick Access Toolbar**.

10. New results are in! Change the value in cell **B5** to **6** and **D5** to **2**. Using the **Quick Access Toolbar**, run the **SortLeague** macro. The *Marketing* team have taken the lead.

11. Remove the **SortLeague** button from the **Quick Access Toolbar**.

12. Save the workbook as **football complete** in a format that will support the running of macros. Then, close it.

> **Note:** A model solution for this activity is provided in the **Sample Solutions** data folder.

8.7 Section Summary

Well done! You have now completed all of the exercises in *Section 8: Macros*. Using the practical knowledge and skills learned you should now be able to:

- Understand macros

- Record a new macro

- Run a macro

- Assign macros to a button on the **Quick Access Toolbar**

- Edit existing macros

- Program a simple new macro from scratch using *Visual Basic* code

- Add comments to a macro to describe its use

- Delete macros

- Print individual macros or all macros in a workbook

> **Note:** Don't worry if you find the idea of writing *Visual Basic* code difficult or confusing. For most situations, *Excel's* recording feature is perfectly adequate. Of course, you will not be expected to write program code manually in your assessment for this qualification.

> **Note:** If you feel you are unsure about any of the topics covered in this section, you should revisit the appropriate exercises and try them again before moving on.

Section 9

Validation and Forms

By the end of this section you should be able to:

Use Data Validation

Restrict Cell Values

Create Input and Error Messages

Use Comments

Protect Workbooks

Insert Form Controls

Use, Create and Test Forms

Assign Macros to Buttons

9.1 Data Validation

Data validation is used to restrict values that can be entered into a cell. This helps to make sure that only valid, expected data appears in a worksheet (known as **data integrity**). If a value does not meet a specific set of conditions, an error message can be displayed.

> **Note:** Data validation is especially useful when creating a spreadsheet for others to use.

Activity:

1. Open the workbook **April Checks**. This worksheet contains a list of *Haunted Castle* maintenance checks performed during the month of *April*.

2. Examine the values in the column **A**. As there are only 30 days in April, any data entered into this column should be restricted to whole numbers between 1 and 30.

3. Select the range **A4:A23**. Then, display the **Data** tab and click the **Data Validation** button in the **Data Tools** group. The **Data Validation** dialog box appears.

4. On the **Settings** tab, under **Validation criteria**, notice that **Any value** is allowed in the selected cells. Expand the **Allow** drop-down list and examine the options available.

5. Select **Whole number**. Then, expand the **Data** drop-down list and examine the various logical operators that can be used. With **between** selected, enter **1** in the **Minimum** box and **30** in the **Maximum** box.

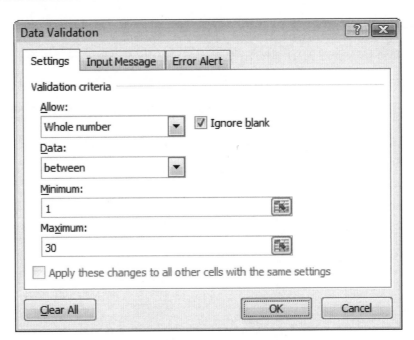

> **Note:** If **Ignore blanks** is selected, cells are allowed to be left empty.

6. Next, display the **Input Message** tab.

> **Note:**   Useful **Input Messages** can appear when a cell restricted by data validation is
> selected. These are ideal for notifying the user of permitted values.

7.   To show a small **Input Message** when a cell in the current range is selected, complete the
      fields as shown below:

> **Note:**   If an invalid value is entered into the current range, a helpful **Error Alert** can also be
> shown.

8.   Display the **Error Alert** tab. To show an error message when an invalid value is entered
      into the current range, complete the fields as shown below:

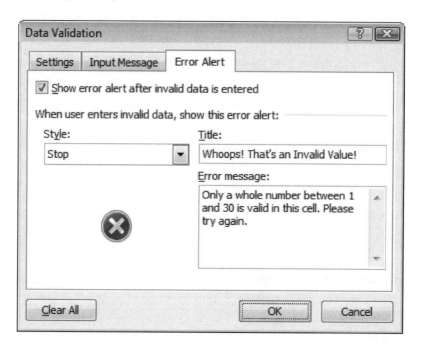

> **Note:** Notice the **Style** drop-down list. Three types of error dialog can be displayed if an invalid value is entered: **Stop** (rejects the value), **Warning** (requests confirmation of the value), and **Information** (allows the value).

9. Click **OK**. Data validation is now applied to the range **A4:A23**. Select any one cell in the range and notice the helpful **Input Message** that appears.

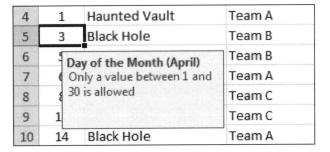

> **Note:** Data validation only applies to new values. Any existing cells containing a value which does not meet the validation criteria will be left untouched.

10. In cell **A17** enter **31** and press **<Enter>**. The value is rejected.

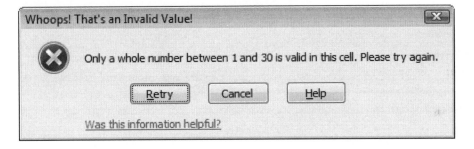

11. Click **Retry** and enter **29**. The value is accepted.

> **Note:** You will create different types of data validation in the next exercise.

12. Save the workbook as **april checks with validation** and leave the file open for the next exercise.

9.2 Advanced Data Validation

Following on from the previous exercise, more advanced types of validation can also be applied to cells such as time, date and text length restrictions. Useful drop-down lists containing the full selection of allowed values can also be used.

Activity:

1. Using the workbook **april checks with validation**, select the range **B4:B23** and display the **Data Validation** dialog box again.

> **Note:**   To make it easier to select a valid entry in the selected range, a drop-down list containing all of the values allowed can be used.

2. On the **Settings** tab, select **List** from the **Allow** drop-down.

3. Click once in the **Source** box. Then, select the range **H7:H11** on the worksheet (the list of 5 attractions, not including the header).

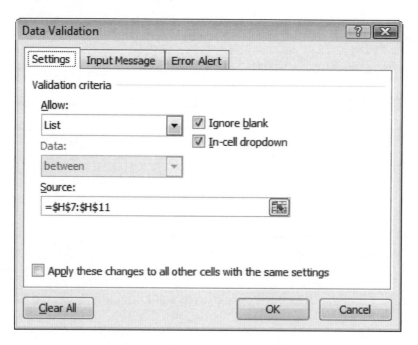

4. On the **Error Alert** tab, select **Warning** from **Style** and enter a **Title** of **Warning! Unknown Attraction**. In the **Error message** box, enter **That attraction is unknown.**

5. Click **OK**. Then, click once in cell **B9** to select it.

6. Enter the value **Bone Shaker** and press <**Enter**>. An error message appears as the value was not on the list of valid attractions. However, as a **Warning** style error alert was used, the user is given the option of continuing with the invalid entry.

7. Select **Cancel**. Then, click the drop-down arrow to the right of the selected cell. From the options shown, select **Tower of Terror**.

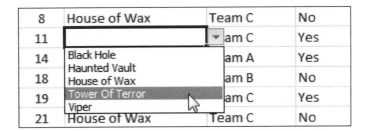

8	House of Wax	Team C	No
11		am C	Yes
14		am A	Yes
18		am B	No
19		am C	Yes
21	House of Wax	Team C	No

8.   For cell **B14** select **Haunted Vault**.

9.   Using data validation, restrict input values for the range **C4:C23**. Allow only **List** items from the range **H14:H16** and display an appropriate **Stop** error alert if an invalid value is entered.

10. Enter **Team D** in cell **C6** and press **<Enter>**. An error alert should appear. Retry and then type **Team B** into the cell. Using the drop-down list for cell **C11**, select **Team A**.

11. Next, apply data validation to the range **D4:D23**. Allow only **Time** values **between 09:00** and **17:00** (the working hours of the maintenance team).

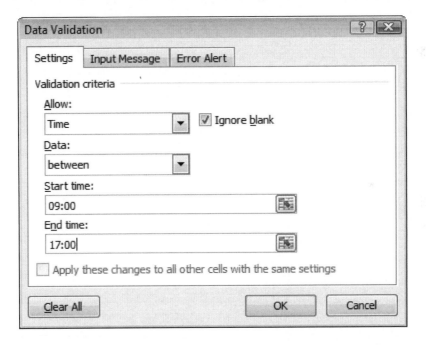

12. Make sure an appropriate **Warning** error alert is displayed if an invalid value is entered.

13. In cell **D8**, enter a time of **04:30** and press **<Enter>**. An error alert should appear. Click **No** and then type the correct value, **16:30**, into the cell.

14. In cell **D15**, enter a time of **08:30** and press **<Enter>**. An error alert should appear. However, **Team A** started early that morning and this is a valid entry. Click **Yes**.

15. Using data validation, restrict input values for the range **F4:F23**. Start by only allowing values with a **Text length** of **less than** a **Maximum** of **30** characters.

16. Display an appropriate **Input Message** which informs the user that no more than 30 characters are allowed. Then, display a **Stop** error alert if an invalid value is entered.

17. In cell **F8**, enter the following text: **Awaiting spare components from factory**.

18. Press **<Enter>** and an error alert appears.

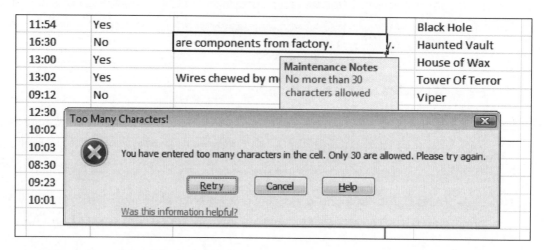

19. Click **Retry** and change the text to the following: **Awaiting spare components**. This text value contains fewer than 30 characters and is allowed.

20. Save the workbook and leave it open for the next exercise.

9.3 Adding Comments

Comments are short pieces of text that can be attached to a cell. They are really useful for adding helpful remarks or additional descriptions to a spreadsheet for other users to read. Normally, comments are not displayed on the worksheet but appear in small pop-up boxes. To help you spot them, a small **comment indicator** (a red triangle) shows where the comments are.

Activity:

1. Using the workbook **april checks with validation**, select the cell **H6**.

2. To attach a comment to this cell, display the **Review** tab and click **New Comment** from the **Comments** group. A new, blank comment appears.

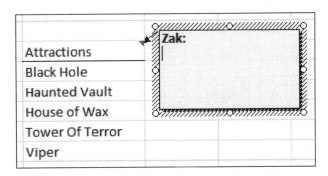

> **Note:**   Notice that your default *Microsoft Office* username appears in the comment box. This can be easily edited or removed if needed.

3. Enter the comment: **Only the 5 major Haunted Castle attractions shown.**

4. Select any other cell and the comment box is closed. However, a comment indicator (a red triangle) appears in the upper right corner of **H6** to indicate a hidden comment.

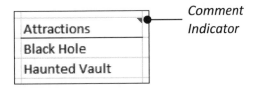

> **Note:**   If the red triangle indicators do not appear, click the **File** tab and then **Options**. Select the **Advanced** section, scroll down to **Display** and make sure **Indicators only, and comments on hover** is selected.

5. Without clicking, place your mouse pointer over cell **H6** and the comment box pops-up again.

6. Add another comment to cell **H13** which reads: **Teams C and D have been merged to form a new Team C.**

7. Click the **Show All Comment**s button in the **Comments** group. All comments are shown.

8.   Save the workbook using the same file name and close it.

9.   Next, open the workbook **Attendance**. Two cells on the worksheet have red triangles which indicate comments. Use the **Show All Comments** button to display them both.

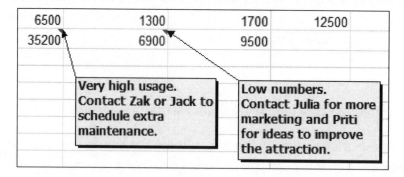

> **Note:**   Comments can be included in print-outs as shown on the worksheet or as a list at the end.

10.   Display the **File** tab and click **Print**. Click **Page Setup** (found at the bottom of **Settings**) to display the **Page Setup** dialog box.

11.   Display the **Sheet** tab in the dialog box and expand the **Comments** drop-down list.

12.   Select **As displayed on sheet** and click **OK**. Observe the effect.

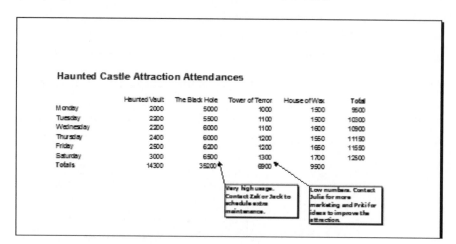

> **Note:**   You may need to adjust paper orientation or scaling to fit everything onto 1 page.

13.   Display the **Page Setup** dialog box again and, using the **Sheet** tab's **Comments** drop-down button, select **At end of sheet**.

14.   Click **OK** and observe the effect – a new page containing all comments is included at the end (use the **Next Page** button to see this).

15.   Click the **Show All Comments** button again to hide all comments.

16.   Save the workbook as **attendance with comments** and close it.

9.4 Protecting Workbooks

As well as adding a password to a workbook to prevent unauthorised access, you can also **protect** specific parts of it. This allows other people to view and use a spreadsheet but limits their ability to make changes.

Activity:

1. Open the workbook **Sensitive**. This spreadsheet contains employee information that you are required to keep private and confidential.

2. Display the **File** tab and click the **Protect Worksheet** button. The options shown allow you to protect the contents of your workbook in a number of different ways. The first four are the most commonly used.

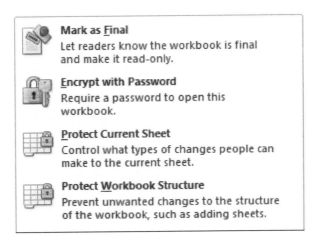

3. Examine the options available and then click **Encrypt with Password** to display the **Encrypt Document** dialog box. Enter the password **bigplanet12345**.

Note: Encryption is the name given to the process of scrambling the contents of a file so that it cannot be opened without permission. It is a useful technique for protecting sensitive documents that you store on portable storage media or send via email.

4. Click **OK**. When prompted, enter the password again (this is to check that you entered it correctly first time) and then click **OK**. The workbook is now password protected.

---

5. Save changes to the workbook and then close it.

6. Next, try to open the workbook **Sensitive** again. You are asked to enter a password in order to open the file. Unless you enter the correct password, it is impossible to open and view the file's contents.

7. Enter the password **bigplanet12345** and click **OK**.

8. To remove the password protection from the workbook, display the **Encrypt Document** dialog box again, delete the password, and then click **OK**.

9. Next, to prevent changes to the workbook's structure (and stop any worksheet additions or deletions), display the **Protect Workbook** drop-down menu on the **File** tab again.

10. Select **Protect Workbook Structure** and examine the **Protect Structure and Windows** dialog box that appears.

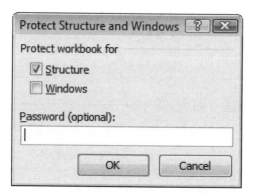

> **Note:** If **Windows** are protected, users will not be able to move or resize worksheet windows within the workbook.

11. With **Structure** selected, enter the password **bigplanet12345** and click **OK**. Then, repeat those actions to confirm. The workbook's structure is now protected.

12. Try adding, deleting, moving or renaming sheets. You are unable to do so.

> **Note:** If a password is not used, anyone can remove the protection by simply using the **Protect Workbook** options on the **File** tab.

13. To prevent changes to the contents of the current worksheet, display the **Protect Workbook** drop-down menu again. Select **Protect Current Sheet** and examine the **Protect Structure** dialog box that appears.

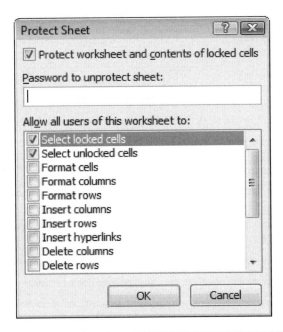

> **Note:** By default, all users of a worksheet are given permission to select cells only. However, notice the other types of permissions that can be granted.

14. Enter the password **bigplanet12345** and confirm. The current worksheet's contents are now protected. Try making changes and read the alert message that appears.

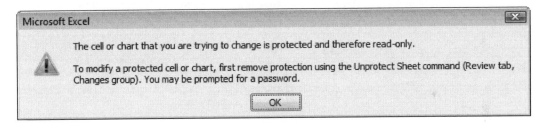

15. Dismiss the alert and display the **Review** tab. Notice that options to protect the current sheet and workbook also appear here in the **Changes** group.

> **Note:** To remove protection from a document, simply display the **Protect Structure and Windows** or **Protect Sheet** dialog boxes again, delete the password, and click **OK**.

16. Remove both the workbook and worksheet protection (using either the options on the **File** tab or on the **Review** tab).

> **Note:** If you have important information on a worksheet, you can **Hide** the whole sheet by right-clicking it's name tab and selecting **Hide**. If **Protect Workbook Structure** is enabled, a user will not be able to **Unhide** and view the data contained.

17. Save changes to the workbook and close it.

9.5 Using Forms

Using a variety of buttons, drop-down lists and option groups (together known as **Controls**), forms can be used to simplify a complex spreadsheet and allow users to interact with it more easily.

Activity:

1. Open the workbook **Registration** (and **Enable Content** if prompted). In this exercise you will complete a simple form created to register new animals at the park's *Jungle Safari*.

2. Examine the form and notice the different types of information requested.

3. An injured, three-year-old male hedgehog has been delivered to the park. It will remain in captivity until it is fit enough to look after itself, at which point it will be released back into the wild. Enter **Hedgehog** into the merged cell **C5:F5**.

4. Next, select **Mammal** from the **Class of Animal** drop-down list. This type of *control* is more commonly known as a **Combo box**.

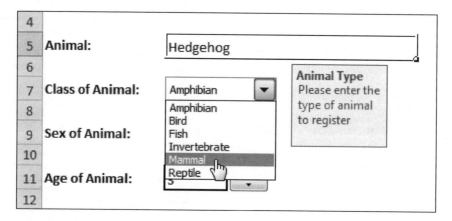

> **Note:** Only allowing predefined values to be selected helps to ensure data integrity.

5. Select **Male** from the **Sex of Animal** control. Then, use the up and down **Spin Buttons** to increase the **Age of Animal** value in cell **C11** to **3**.

6. Next, notice the 7 controls shown in the range **A14:I17**. These are called **Option Buttons** and *only 1* can be selected at a time. Experiment by selecting each item in the group and observe the effect. When you are finished, select **Europe**.

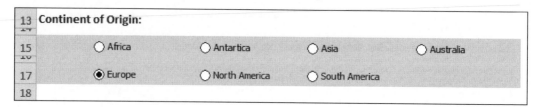

7. The four controls shown in the range **A21:I21** are called **Check Boxes**. Each one can either by selected (checked) or not. Select the first two only.

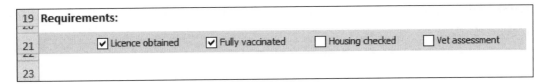

8. To the right of the **Assigned Handler** label in cell **H5** is an example of a **List Box** control. Unlike a **Combo Box**, the items contained are shown without needing to drop-down a list. Select **John**.

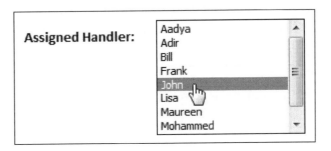

Note: Although the feature is not enabled here, it is possible to allow **List Boxes** to have more than one item selected at a time.

9. Display the **Record** worksheet. This has been set up to show all of the selections made on the **New Animal Registration Form** worksheet.

10. Return to the **New Animal Registration Form** worksheet and locate the large **Button** labelled **Print**.

Note: As you will see later in this exercise, assigning a macro to a form button is just as easy as assigning a macro to a **Quick Access Toolbar** button.

11. A macro which prints the contents of the **Record** worksheet has been created and assigned to the **Print** button. Click the **Print** button now and observe the results.

12. Experiment with changing the values of the various form features on the **New Animal Registration Form** worksheet. Notice that all changes are repeated on the **Record** worksheet.

13. When you are finished, close the workbook without saving.

9.6 Working with Buttons

Buttons are probably the most commonly used form control available in *Excel*. Once added to a worksheet, they can be programmed to run a macro when clicked. They also appear floating *above* the cells and can be placed anywhere you like.

Activity:

1. Create a new, blank workbook. Then, display the **Developer** tab on the **Ribbon**.

> **Note:** If the **Developer** tab is not visible, display the **File** tab and click **Options**. On the **Excel Options** screen that appears, select **Customise Ribbon**. In the **Main Tabs** list on the right, check **Developer** and click **OK**.

2. Click the **Insert** button in the **Controls** group and examine the **Form Controls** that appear.

> **Note:** **ActiveX Controls** are similar to **Form Controls** but offer more features for advanced users.

3. Rest your mouse pointer over each item (*without* clicking) and observe the **ToolTip** that appears. When you are finished, select **Button**.

4. The mouse pointer changes to a crosshair, ✛, when placed over the worksheet. Click and drag to draw a **frame** in the centre of the worksheet (approximately two cells wide by three cells high).

5. Release the mouse button and the **Assign Macro** dialog box appears. For now, click **Cancel** (you will create and assign a macro later). A new button appears.

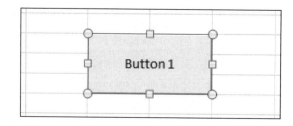

---

6. Click the text **Button 1** to start editing the button's label. Change this to **Insert Name**.

7. To confirm the change, click away from the button (<**Enter**> will create a new line).

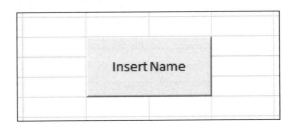

8. Select cell **B2**. Then, start recording a new **Macro** with **Use Relative References** selected. Name it **InsertName**.

9. As the macro is recording, enter your name in the current cell and press <**Enter**>. Then, stop recording the macro.

10. Right-click the new button control and select **Assign Macro**. Select **InsertName** from the **Macro name** list and click **OK**. The macro is now assigned to the button.

11. Select cell **B4**. Click the **Insert Name** button and the macro is run, entering your name into the currently active cell. Using the **Insert Name** button, experiment by running this macro in other cells.

> **Note:**   Left mouse clicks are usually used to interact with a form control. However, to edit the control and show its resize handles, it must be right-clicked.

12. Right-click to start editing the **Insert Name** button. Then, by dragging its border, move it around the worksheet.

13. Next, try using the resize handles to increase and decrease its size.

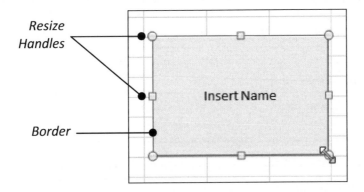

> **Note:**   All other form controls can be added, moved, resized and repositioned using the techniques described in this exercise.

14. Save the workbook as **button control** (using a macro-enabled file format) and close it.

9.7 Creating a Form

Using the same techniques to insert, position and resize a button on a worksheet, many other form controls can be created and combined to construct a useful, user-friendly interface.

> **Note:**   Creating forms can be tricky. Read and follow the instructions below carefully.

Activity:

1. Open the workbook **Requisition**. This spreadsheet features an incomplete **New Computer Request Form** which will be used to create a printed **Order Confirmation**.

2. Examine the formulas used in column **K**. Cells **K8** and **K9** feature **Lookup** functions that use the value stored in **G7** to find information stored in the **Item Data** worksheet. Cells **K12**, **K16**, **K17** and **K18** use **IF** functions with the values stored in column **G**.

> **Note:**   You will see why formulas in column **K** refer to values in column **G** later.

3. First, use the **Insert** button on the **Developer** tab to create a new **Combo Box**. Resize and reposition it so it fits neatly within cell **C7**, as shown below.

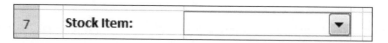

> **Note:**   To select a form control in order to edit it, *right-click* it once.

4. With the control selected (and the resize handles on show), click the **Properties** button in the **Control** group on the **Ribbon**. The **Format Control** dialog box appears.

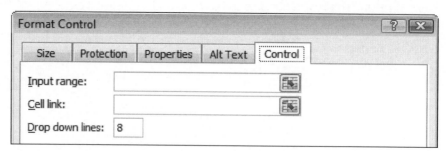

> **Note:**   The **Collapse/Expand** button, ⊞, can be used to reduce the size of the dialog.

5. **Input range** is used to select a range of values to place in the **Combo Box**. Click once in the **Input range** box, then display the **Item Data** worksheet and select **C4:C13**.

> **Note:**   When an item is selected in the **Combo Box**, the **index** of the selection appears in the **Cell link** cell as a whole number. The index is the position that the selected item appears in the list (e.g. 1 = first item, 2 = second item, and so on).

6. Click once in the **Cell link** box. Then, select the cell **G7** on the **Request Form** worksheet.

7. Finally, change the value in **Drop down lines** to **10** to show 10 items when clicked.

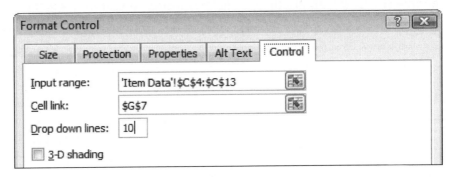

8. Click **OK**. Then, click away from the new **Combo Box** to deselect it.

9. Try the **Combo Box** by clicking its drop-down arrow button and selecting **Printer**. Notice that the value **5** appears in cell **G7** – the **Cell link** cell – representing the index of the selected item (**Printer** is the fifth item in the **Combo Box's** list).

10. Try selecting other values in the **Combo Box** and observe the effect. As the **Lookup** functions in cells **K8** and **K9** use the value in **G7**, their values are automatically updated.

11. Next, insert a **Spin Button** and resize and reposition it so it fits neatly within cell **E9**, as shown below.

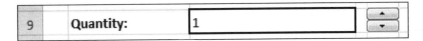

12. With the control selected, click the **Properties** button in the **Control** group on the **Ribbon**. The **Format Control** dialog box appears again.

13. Set the **Current value** to **1**, the **Minimum value** to **1**, and the **Maximum value** to **20**. Click once in the **Cell link** box and then select cell **C9** on the worksheet.

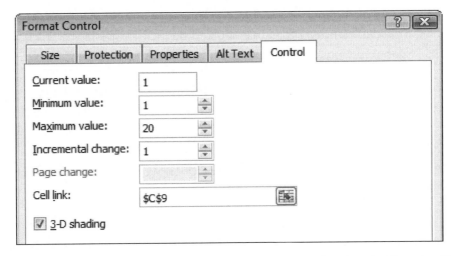

14. Click **OK**. Then, click away from the new **Spin Button** to deselect it. Now try the new control by clicking the up and down arrows on the **Spin Button**. Notice that the value in cell **C9** (the **Cell link** cell) changes.

> **Note:**   Notice also that the value in **C9** is limited to whole numbers between 1 and 20.

15. Next, insert *two* **Option Buttons** and resize and reposition them so that they both fit neatly, side by side, within cell **C12**. Edit the text of the first **Option Button** to **Yes** and the second to **No**, as shown below.

12	Include VAT?	⦿ Yes ◯ No

> **Note:**   *Excel* automatically groups **Option Buttons** so that they work together.

16. Select the **Option Button** labelled **Yes** and display the **Format Control** dialog box. Make sure **Checked** is selected and then click once in the **Cell link** box. Select cell **G12** on the worksheet and click **OK**.

17. Select the **Option Button** labelled **No** and display the **Format Control** dialog box. Notice that **Unchecked** is already selected and the **Cell link** box is set to **$G$12** again. Click **OK**.

18. Click away from the new **Option Buttons** to deselect them. Now try the new controls by selecting **Yes** or **No**. Notice that the index value in cell **G12** (the **Cell link**) changes. As the **IF** function in cell **K12** uses the value in **G12**, this value is also automatically updated.

19. Next, insert a **Check Box** and resize and reposition it neatly within cell **C14**. Edit the text to **Require Signature**. Then, insert a **Check Box** labelled **Next Day Delivery** in **C15** and another labelled **Include Software** in **C16**, as shown below.

14	Delivery Options:	☐ Require Signature
15		☐ Next Day Delivery
16		☐ Include Software

20. Select the **Check Box** labelled **Require Signature** and display the **Format Control** dialog box. Make sure **Unchecked** is selected and then click once in the **Cell link** box. Select cell **G14** on the worksheet and click **OK**.

21. Perform the same steps for the **Check Box** labelled **Next Day Delivery**, selecting a **Cell link** of **G15**. Do the same for the **Include Software**, selecting a **Cell link** of **G16**.

22. Click away from the new check boxes to deselect them. Now try the new controls and notice the values that appear in **G14:G16**. As the **IF** functions in **K16:K18** use these values, these are also automatically updated.

23. Finally, record a new macro that sets the **Print Area** to **H1:M20** and prints the **Order Confirmation**. Assign this new macro the **Create Order Confirmation button**.

24. Using the **View** tab, hide the workbook's **Gridlines**.

25. Save the workbook as **requisition complete** with *macros enabled* and leave it open.

9.8 Testing a Form

Once you have created a new form, you should always test it thoroughly to check that it works as expected.

Activity:

1. The **requisition complete** workbook should still be open. You have received a new computer request from *Fiona* at reception – let's use this to test the new form:

    I would like to order 3 new laptops please. I pay VAT and would like next day delivery. As this order is valuable I will need to sign to receive it. Thanks, Fiona.

2. Enter **1** in **C5** and then complete the **New Computer Request Form** using the data provided by *Fiona*. When you click the **Create Order Confirmation** button, the following **Order Confirmation** receipt should be printed.

Order Confirmation

Order Number:	**1**
Date of Order:	29/11/2012
Item Purchased:	Laptop Computer
Cost:	£450.00
Quantity:	3
Subtotal:	£1,350.00
VAT:	£270.00
Total:	£1,620.00
Require Signature:	*Yes*
Next Day Delivery:	*Yes*
Include Software:	*No*

Note: If your **Order Confirmation** does not appear as shown, you should check your form for errors. To help, a model solution is available in the **Sample Solutions** folder.

3. Save the workbook using the same file name and close it.

Note: You will learn more about testing spreadsheets in the next section.

9.9 Develop Your Skills

At the end of every section you will find a *Develop Your Skills* activity. Work through it to ensure you have fully understood the previous exercises and can demonstrate the practical skills learned.

1. Open the workbook **Kitchen**. This spreadsheet features a price list for kitchen items used for furnishing *Big Planet Theme Park* hotel suites.

2. Use suitable data validation with cell **C3** to encourage users to keep values to a text length of less than or equal to 20 characters (but can be more if absolutely needed). Include a suitable **Input Message** and an **Error Alert** with a **Warning** style.

3. Use data validation to restrict the values that can be entered into cell **C4**. Only whole numbers between **1** and **1000** should be allowed. Use a suitable **Input Message** and **Error Alert** with a **Stop** style.

4. Use data validation to restrict the values that can be entered into the cell range **D8:D49**. Only whole numbers between **0** and **100** should be allowed (ignoring blank values is fine). Use a suitable **Input Message** and **Error Alert** with a **Stop** style.

5. Insert a **Combo Box** in **C5**. Set the **Input range** to use the list of **Kitchen Types** on the **Types** worksheet and set the **Link cell** to **D5**. Reduce the **Drop down** lines to **5**.

6. To test the pricing of the units, select a **Style of Units** other than **None**. Formulas to calculate **Price** and **Total Price**, using the value in **D5**, have already been entered.

7. Place the following order for **Priti Rajan**, reference **123**, for **Teak** style units:

Ref	Unit	Quantity
1	BASE HL	3
6	BASE DL	2
12	DRAWER PACK	5
24	WALL UNITS 900	5

> **Note:** The total value of the order should be **£2,538**.

8. Create a new macro that uses an **AutoFilter** to show only items that have a **Quantity** value greater than 0. The macro should print the form and then turn off the **AutoFilter**.

9. Place a **Button** at the top of the form that runs the new macro and test it works.

10. Protect the document using the password **bigplanet12345**, and then save it as **kitchen complete** in a format that will support the running of macros. Then, close it.

> **Note:** A model solution for this activity is provided in the **Sample Solutions** data folder.

9.10 Section Summary

Well done! You have now completed all of the exercises in *Section 9: Validation and Forms*. Using the practical knowledge and skills learned you should now be able to:

- Use data validation to check and restrict data entry values

- Create input and error messages to help users

- Insert and delete comments

- Protect workbooks and worksheets

- Insert controls (e.g. **Buttons**, **Combo Boxes**, **Check Boxes**, **Lists**, **Option Buttons** and **Spin Buttons**).

- Assign macros to buttons

- Use controls to build forms

- Understand the importance of testing forms

> **Note:** If you feel you are unsure about any of the topics covered in this section, you should revisit the appropriate exercises and try them again before moving on.

Section 10

Design and Test

By the end of this section you should be able to:

Interpret User Requirements

Design and Create Professional Solutions

Check and Correct Formulas

Create and Use Test Plans

10.1 User Requirements

Before creating a spreadsheet to model and solve a problem, it is always important to stop and consider its design. How will it work, what data and formulas are needed, what are the expected inputs and outputs, and how will it meet all of the user requirements? In particular, it is important that the spreadsheet is "fit-for-purpose" and is clearly organised and easy-to-use.

Activity:

1. *John* at the park's *IT Centre* has asked you to create a spreadsheet to work out the *total* pay for all of his department's staff. Each person's wage is calculated as the number of hours worked multiplied by their hourly rate. If that person works overtime, this is paid at "time and a half".

> **Note:** "Time and a half" is calculated as 1.5 times normal hourly rate.

2. Design a new spreadsheet to model *John's* "brief" (his list of requirements), and calculate the weekly pay for the following staff members:

Staff No.	Name	Basic Rate	Hours Worked	Normal Hours
1001	Michael Johnson	£10.00	37	37
1002	Glyn Jones	£11.50	39	30
1006	Sami Amir	£9.75	41	37
1010	Christina McCaffrey	£14.00	39	40

> **Note:** A spreadsheet is only as useful as the information and formulas you enter into it. Take care when you are given data and enter it correctly and accurately.

3. To present the data clearly include suitable labels and cell formatting. Then, enter all necessary formulas to calculate each person's pay, including column totals.

4. If the final total for all staff pay is not **£1,835.50** you have done something wrong. Go back and examine your spreadsheet and find the error.

5. Include conditional formatting to highlight any **Hours Worked** that include more than 5 hours of overtime.

> **Note:** A model solution for this activity is provided in the **Sample Solutions** data folder. This is the professional standard expected by *John*. How does yours compare?

6. Save the workbook as **staff pay** and close it.

10.2 Design Tips

A well-designed spreadsheet should be easy to use and allow you (or others) to enter and extract information quickly and accurately. So, when creating your own spreadsheets, try to consider the following points of good practice:

* Always take care when designing the structure of your spreadsheet. It is a good idea to keep all relevant worksheets in the same workbook.

* Always analyse the requirements for a spreadsheet in detail _before_ starting to build it. What information will be recorded and what outputs are required? This will help you to identify any rows, columns, functions, formulas and charts needed.

* Use meaningful column and row labels (and **AutoFit** columns to avoid wasted space). This helps you and others to understand the contents of a spreadsheet quickly and easily.

* When creating lists or tables of information, it is generally best to organise data in rows below appropriate column header labels. This makes it easier to sort, filter and analyse.

* Try to avoid leaving unnecessary blank rows in a table or list of information. This can confuse _Excel's_ automatic filtering and sorting features.

* Use the correct cell data types to give you more control over how values are presented.

* Use data validation, drop-down lists and input/error messages wherever possible. This helps to guide the user and reduces the risk of entering invalid values.

* To prevent users of a spreadsheet from deleting important data or introducing errors, consider protecting cells and workbook structure.

* Use functions wherever possible rather than long, complex and error-prone formulas.

* If your spreadsheet contains sensitive information, always use a strong password to protect it. This is especially important when sending files by e-mail or when placing them on a removable storage device (that may get lost).

* Try to assign macros to buttons on a worksheet. This highlights their existence and allows you to create a more user-friendly experience.

* Ask colleagues or users for their opinions when developing a spreadsheet. Do they experience any problems storing and extracting data?

* Apply simple text and cell formatting to highlight important information and give your spreadsheets a more professional appearance.

* Use cell formatting to make it obvious where users of a spreadsheet should enter data.

* Test your spreadsheet solutions thoroughly to make sure that the data they store, manipulate and present is correct, accurate and "fit for purpose".

10.3 Checking Formulas

Spreadsheets are not much use if the formulas within them contain errors. All formulas within worksheets should be checked thoroughly to make sure that you have entered them correctly and that they produce the *expected* results.

In some cases *Excel* will warn you that a formula is incorrect. If so, a formula error value starting with a # (hash) symbol is displayed in the relevant cell:

#NULL!	The ranges specified in your formula are incorrect
#DIV/0!	You tried to divide by 0 and this is not allowed
#VALUE!	You tried to apply a calculation with data of the wrong type
#REF!	Cell references are not valid or are missing
#NAME?	A function's name has been mistyped
#NUM!	The result created by a formula is too big
#N/A	A value referenced in your formula is missing
######	The result is too long to fit into a cell

Activity:

1. Open the workbook **Totals**. This spreadsheet shows monthly visitors to the park's *Haunted Castle* attraction in a six month period. Unfortunately, it also contains a number of errors which must be corrected before the results can be trusted and relied upon.

> **Note:** Notice the green triangles that appear in the top left corner of certain cells, ◤. These indicate *possible* errors in the formulas for those cells.

2. Click once in cell **B5**. This cell contains the error **#VALUE!** indicating that the formula is using data of the wrong type.

3. Notice the **Trace Error** button that has appeared beside the selected cell, ◇. Place your mouse pointer over this button without clicking to see a brief description of the error.

	Month 1	Month 2	Month 3	Month 4	Month 5
visitors	200	300	400	-100	150
◇ ▾	#VALUE!	300	700	600	750

A value used in the formula is of the wrong data type.

4. Double click in the cell. The formula is shown within the cell itself, with coloured borders indicating the ranges used in the calculation (this is a really useful way of checking the cells referenced by a formula). Can you see what the error is?

5. The formula is trying to add the label in **A5** to the value in **B4**. Edit the formula so that it simply reads **=B4** and press <**Enter**>. The error value disappears and **200** is shown in **B5**.

6. Next, click once in cell **H4** and read the brief description on the **Trace Error** button.

7. *Excel* has detected that the formula contains an unknown function name and has displayed the **#NAME?** error value in the cell. Can you see what the error is?

8. The function **SUM** has been spelled incorrectly. Correct this and press <**Enter**> to remove the error value.

9. The result appears as **0**, which is clearly not correct. Double click **H4** to see the range that the formula refers to.

Month 1	Month 2	Month 3	Month 4	Month 5	Month 6	Total	Ave
200	300	400	-100	150	500	=SUM(B7:G7)	
200	300	700	600	750	750	SUM(number1,	
0	0	0	0	0	0		

10. The range **B7:G7** is not correct. You could edit the formula in the cell, but instead try dragging and dropping the blue range rectangle to the correct location, as shown below.

Month 1	Month 2	Month 3	Month 4	Month 5	Month 6	Total	Ave
200	300	400	-100	150	500	=SUM(B7:G7)	
200	300	700	600	750	750	SUM(number1,	

Note: You can also click and drag the corners of the blue range rectangle to expand or contract it.

---

11. Press <**Enter**> to confirm the change. The correct formula now produces the result **1450**.

12. Next, click once in cell **I4** and read the brief description on the **Trace Error** button. *Excel* has detected that the formula is trying to divide by **0** and has displayed the **#DIV/0!** error.

Note: In computing, dividing by zero is not possible and will always produce an error.

---

13. As there are six months worth of data, the formula should divide by **6** in order to get the monthly average. Correct this now by editing the formula in the **Formula Bar**.

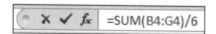

14. Press <**Enter**> to confirm the change. The average formula is now correct.

15. Unfortunately, cell **I4** now contains the error **#####**. This simply means that the cell is too small to display the value contained. Increase the size of column **I** to correct this.

16. Next, notice that the range **B7:G7** contains references to values on another worksheet. Delete the worksheet **Sheet2** and observe the effect.

17. The **#REF!** error appears indicating bad cell references. Select cell **B7** and link this cell to the value in cell **B4** on the **Expected** worksheet.

18. Copy this corrected cell to the range **C7:G7**.

> **Note:** It is important to perform simple visual inspections on your spreadsheets to check that amounts tally and that the results of formulas are as expected.

19. Although all of the errors that *Excel* warned you about have now been corrected, there are still a few errors remaining in this spreadsheet. Can you find them?

20. Firstly, the cell **C5** should add the contents of **B5** and **C4**. Correct this now.

21. Next, cell **G5** is a copy of **F5**. Correct this now.

22. The cumulative total in cell **G5** now matches the final total in **H4**, which is correct.

23. The value in **E4** does not make sense! You cannot have **-100** visitors. This should be **100**, so correct the error now.

24. Although not strictly an error, the **Average per month** value does not need to be displayed to 10 decimal places. Format the cell to display the result to **2 Decimal places** instead.

25. The spreadsheet is now complete and correct. Compare your final spreadsheet to that shown below and check that all of your calculations are correct.

First Half Cumulative Totals								
	Month 1	Month 2	Month 3	Month 4	Month 5	Month 6	Total	Average per month
Number of Haunted Castle visitors	200	300	400	100	150	500	1650	275.00
Cumulative Total	200	500	900	1000	1150	1650		
Expected	150	250	500	300	300	400		

> **Note:** A useful feature of *Excel* is the **Error Checking** facility on the **Formulas** tab. This steps you through each error in a spreadsheet one at a time.

26. Save the workbook as **final totals** and close it.

10.4 Creating a Test Plan

To test the functionality of a spreadsheet and check that it works in different conditions, it is often a good idea to develop a **test plan**. This features a table of "dummy" (made up) _input_ values that cover a wide range of normal, unlikely and extreme scenarios.

> **Note:** It is impossible to test the result of entering all possible values into a spreadsheet. However, a good developer will try to consider the many ways that a spreadsheet could go wrong and then take steps to prevent it (i.e. by using data validation).

Activity:

1. Open the workbook **Testing**. This spreadsheet records gift sales in the highlighted range **B4:B8**. It calculates the difference from the average and the percentage of total sales for each member of staff. Anyone with above average sales will receive a 10% bonus.

2. Study the worksheet. Double-click each cell containing a formula to check it and make sure all cell references are correct.

3. Display the **Test Plan** worksheet and examine its contents. The table outlines 6 sets of data that can be applied to the **Sales** worksheet to test its functionality. This includes many different eventualities, both normal and abnormal.

Test Plan						
			Test Cases			
Salesperson	Set #1	Set #2	Set #3	Set #4	Set #5	Set #6
Smith	-1	ten	0	0.1	10.001	10000
Brown	-0.1	brown	0	0.01	456.78	999.99
Mohammed	-2	m	1	0.001	100	500
Singh	-50	!	2	0.2	29.99	10000000
Chapman	-1000	1b	3	0.939	499.27	456.5

> **Note:** Test values that explore the "bounds" of what is acceptable and what is not can often expose errors in a spreadsheet. For example, a cell that is only allowed to accept numbers between **1** and **5** can be tested using the following dummy values: **0, 0.9, 1, 1.1, 4, 4.9, 5, 5.1, 6**, etc.

4. Starting with **Set #1**, enter the values given into **B4:B8** on the **Sales** worksheet. Are the results as expected? If not, changes to the spreadsheet will be needed.

5. Mark each test set as having passed or not on the **Test Plan** worksheet (**C12:H12**). You can make comments in the **Notes** area to describe the results of each test. When all tests have been completed you can be confident that the spreadsheet is ready to be used.

6. Save the workbook as **testing complete** and close it.

10.5 Develop Your Skills

At the end of every section you will find a *Develop Your Skills* activity. Work through it to ensure you have fully understood the previous exercises and can demonstrate the practical skills learned.

1. Consider the following user requirements:

    I need a new spreadsheet that will record cash flow for one week of sales at the *Rumbling Bellies* restaurant.

    The data for all seven days of the week should be displayed on one spreadsheet.

    Each day of the week will need to record an opening balance and a calculated closing balance.

    For each day of the week, the cash received and cash paid out or banked will need to be manually input.

    The profit or loss made each day also needs to be calculated (i.e. cash in minus cash out).

    The closing balance for one day will become the opening balance for the next day.

    Each day must include the name of the person entering the data.

2. Design and produce a spreadsheet that models the user requirements given, including any suitable formatting, data types, formulas, validation and cell protection.

3. Develop a test plan with dummy data and thoroughly check the spreadsheet for possible problems. Remember to use lots of test values that explore the normal, extreme and boundaries of permitted values.

4. Save the workbook as **cash flow** and then close it.

5. Open the workbook **Wages**. This spreadsheet shows the pay calculations for a cleaning squad of 4 people. They are paid an hourly rate for the number of hours they work with 50% extra for overtime.

6. Unfortunately the spreadsheet contains a number of formula errors. Find and correct them all (the final **Net Pay Total** in **F10** should be **£1,000.25**).

7. Save the workbook as **wages complete** and then close *Excel*.

> **Note:**   Model solutions for this activity are provided in the **Sample Solutions** data folder.

10.6 Section Summary

Well done! You have now completed all of the exercises in *Section 10: Design and Test*. Using the practical knowledge and skills learned you should now be able to:

- Interpret spreadsheet requirements from a user brief

- Design spreadsheet solutions to solve a problem

- Check and correct formulas

- Create meaningful test plans

- Use test plans to test a spreadsheet

> **Note:**   If you feel you are unsure about any of the topics covered in this section, you should revisit the appropriate exercises and try them again before moving on.

Next Steps

You have now completed all of the sections in this guide. If you are unsure about any of the topics covered, please revisit the appropriate exercises and try them again before undertaking the assessment for this unit.

If you are interested in exploring some of *Microsoft Excel's* more powerful features, why not use the Internet to find out more about the following advanced topics:

Feature	Description
Templates	*Excel's* templates work in much the same way as *Word's* document templates. Any normal workbook can be saved as a template, allowing you to create a standard layout that can be used as a basis for future spreadsheets.
Charts	There are many chart types available in *Excel*. Build on the basic lessons learned in Section 5 and explore some of the other styles available, including **Area, Doughnut, Bubble, Surface** and **Radar**.
Sparklines	Find out more about *Excel 2010's* interesting new **Sparklines** feature, which lets you place small "micro-charts" within one or more cells. They are great for showing trend information quickly and easily.
Functions	Expand on the lessons learned in Section 4 and learn to recognise and use all of the various functions available in *Excel*.
Tracking	It is very common to have another person review and edit spreadsheets that you create. If a workbook has been set up to "track changes", any changes made to a worksheet will be recorded. Once you get the updated workbook back you can then accept or reject each change.
PivotTables	A **PivotTable** is a powerful feature of *Excel* that organises and then summarises large amounts of data. In many ways it is similar to the sorting and filtering features you have already seen in this guide, but it allows for much more control over how the data is displayed.
Forms	Build on the lessons learned in Section 9 and explore some of the added functionality that forms can bring to a spreadsheet.
Visual Basic	To make the most out of macros and forms it helps to be able to understand and edit **Visual Basic** code.
Naming Ranges	To allow you to refer to a range of cells more easily, you can give it a name using *Excel's* **Name** box (see Exercise 1.1). You can then refer to this name instead of the range reference in formulas and functions.

Other Products

CiA Training is a leading publishing company which has consistently delivered the highest quality products since 1985. Our experienced in-house publishing team has developed a wide range of flexible and easy to use self-teach resources for individual learners and corporate clients all over the world. Supporting many popular qualifications including *ECDL, CLAIT, ITQ, Functional Skills* and *Cambridge Nationals*, our products are an invaluable asset to tutors and training managers seeking support for their programme delivery.

At the time of publication we currently offer materials for:

* Cambridge Nationals in ICT

* Functional Skills

* ITQ Level 1, Level 2 and Level 3

* New CLAIT, CLAIT Plus and CLAIT Advanced

* ECDL and ECDL Advanced

* CiA Revision Series

* Start IT

* Skill for Life in ICT

* e-Citizen

* Open Learning Guides

* CourseNotes

* Trainers Packs

* And many, many more...

> Note: *CiA Training* learning resources are available in individual printed book format or as a site licence in editable *Microsoft Word* format.

We hope you have enjoyed using this guide and would love to hear your opinions about our materials. To let us know how we are doing and to get up-to-the-minute information on our current range of products, please visit us online at:

www.ciatraining.co.uk

Index